MW00491316

LIFE IN TRANSITION

Life in Transition
ESSAYS AND DIVERSIONS

KAREN GILDEN

Artha Press 2019

Published in the United States by Artha Press 2019

Paperback ISBN 978-1-886922-04-4
Library of Congress Control Number: 2019904527

Cover design by Joanne McClennan
Cover photograph by Ray Gilden © 2011
Author photograph by Melina Gilden © 2019

Printed in the United States of America
Artha Press
Portland, Oregon 97210

To Ray, with love

CONTENTS

PREFACE

In his preface to *Essays of E.B.White,* the author writes "some people . . . feel that it is presumptuous of a writer to assume that his little excursions or his small observations will interest the reader. There is some justice in their complaint." I would never argue about writing with E. B. White, and indeed I can only agree. Writing personal essays is rather presumptuous.

I was a freelance writer for about 20 years, always working to understand a publication's market and an editor's requests. When blogging appeared I was eager to take it up, seeing it as a chance to finally write what I wanted, without the pressure of an editor's demands, or even writer's guidelines.

That there is danger in such an undertaking is clear, and one is apt to make a fool of oneself fairly often. It is, as White says, an escape from discipline.

The essays included here are drawn primarily from my blog, Random Vectors, begun in 2006.

Though I always meant to write regularly, it was hit and miss, depending on where we were and what we were doing. Many of the pieces are from the three and a half years we lived in Sisters, Oregon, a place and a time that inspired me.

These "small observations" are reflections of my life, and to better tell the story I've included pieces from *Tea & Bee's Milk,* co-authored with my husband Ray while living in Turkey for a year, and excerpts from my book, *Camping With the Communists,* which details our 1977 camping trip through the Soviet Union.

I hope you find them diverting at least, inspirational at best; and hopefully, not too presumptuous.

—*Karen Gilden,*
Portland, Oregon 2019

INTRODUCTION

The book you hold represents my effort to assuage grief. After my husband died I desperately needed a project. I wanted to write, but no subject compelled me and "normal" life felt too remote to make sense of. So I turned to what I had already written, searching out essays for *Life in Transition*.

It was a slow process, but it gave me something to focus on. The result is a kind of autobiography, written across many years in many places. The focus here is on travel, and our mutual love of the outdoors. We had other interests of course, but they are not part of this story.

Because we traveled often and moved often, our life from the outside often looked chaotic, even to close friends. In the hope that I can limit that confusion, and make clearer what follows, I offer this: Ray and I met on a blind date in 1964 in San Jose, California. It was clear from the beginning that travel would be a cornerstone of our life together and our first trip was to Mexico shortly before we married. It was a trip beset with mishaps and trials of patience, mostly of the automotive kind. But we laughed and persevered and by the end we knew we could get through anything together.

We moved from the Bay Area to Eugene, Oregon in 1970—a first hint of our tendency to be gypsies. In 1975 I began studying Russian language and culture at the University of Oregon. This was a long held interest that eventually led the three of us (me, Ray, and 11-year-old Jennifer) to take a six-month circle journey through Europe in a VW camper—including 39 days in the Soviet Union, putting my two years of Russian to the test. It was a trip that reaffirmed in all of us a love of travel and a determination to do more. We returned to Europe for three months in 1981, and for six months in 1987.

In 1990 we moved from Eugene to Portland, Oregon.

In 1993 we visited friends in Turkey on a three week vacation and fell in love with the country and its people. And in 1995 we got an offer we couldn't refuse, so we set off again, to spend a year in Göcek, Turkey.

Between trips we worked and saved for the next one. We were lucky that during most of this time the economy was strong and jobs were plentiful. Ray had a union job that afforded him leaves-of-absence. I worked various jobs, full time and part time, often while freelancing.

After our year in Turkey it was tough to go back to an 8 to 5 job so we postponed that dreary day and traveled a bit more: three months touring Mexico in a secondhand Dodge Colt. Home again, we traded the Colt for a used VW camper and drove across the U.S. on Highway 20, from Newport, Oregon to Boston—a long held dream of Ray's.

Having now spent a good portion of our savings, we moved to Corvallis, Oregon, found jobs, and went back to work. In 2000 we fulfilled another dream and bought a little vacation house in southwest France where we eventually spent six months of each year. But in 2007 a new granddaughter and a collapsing dollar brought us back to the U.S. Three moves later we were back in Portland, and Ray was seriously ill.

No life is free of disappointment and pain, but until Ray's final illness we were both blessed with good health and a curiosity that made almost everything an adventure. Life was challenging but it was almost always fun, and Ray's presence made every destination a home for me. It was a joy to share a life with him. He died February 2, 2018.

RIDING THE SUN

The following two essays were written in response to prompts given in a writer's group. Taken together they explain my life-long fascination with travel, and the curiosity that drove me to explore what I could of our beautiful planet.

Mapping memories

I was born and grew up in California but I didn't see the ocean until I was 12. My first glimpse was of breakers—a long, pale white line against an endless blue—seen through the windshield of a '52 Plymouth. We were still miles away, coming down the slope of California's coastal range and heading toward Crescent City. I was so excited. "Hurry up!" I said, "Drive faster!"

The ocean did not disappoint. But it wasn't the wading, swimming, and sun bathing that attracted me to the beach that summer, though I enjoyed all that. What drew me was the enormity of the sea and what lay beyond it.

I wanted desperately to hitch a ride with the sun and go wherever it was going, and lying on my beach towel I imagined Japan and China and tried to comprehend the great distance that separated us. I asked questions my parents couldn't answer: "When the sun sets here is it already in Japan? Or is it still over the ocean?" and "How long would it take to sail there?" and "What is exactly opposite where we are right now?"

Maps decorated my childhood room and still hang in my office. As a teenager my wish for Christmas was not pretty clothes, but a world globe. I loved maps and I loved the world they described. But it was putting my feet in the ocean that made the world real for me in a way maps never had. The ocean knocked something loose in me and I've been trying to fix it ever since.

Some years ago my husband and daughter and I spent Christmas week on the island of Rhodes. We rented a couple of rooms in Lindos, above a Greek family's home, and had breakfast every morning on a tiny balcony overlooking the sea. And there, for the first time, I saw the sun rise from the sea instead of sink into it. Looking east that first morning I waited to feel something grand; a revelation perhaps, or an intuitive grasp of universal perfection. Nothing. Instead, we ate our breakfast, commented on the oddity, said how lucky we were to have sunshine in the depths of winter, and went for a walk on the beach.

The two memories could serve as bookends to my life. On one end the childhood excitement of an endless future with endless questions waiting to be answered; on the other the sated traveler who recognizes the wonder but can no longer feel it.

That would neatly tie the package but it would sadden me deeply to call it true. My fascination with the world and the maps that plot it continually reinforce my wonder. I no longer wish to ride the sun but I will always be captivated by whatever it illuminates, just over the horizon.

Travel lessons

The poet John Berryman once said, "We must travel in the direction of our fear." He was speaking, I think, about the fear that nibbles away at our self assurance; the fear that cramps our gut, inhibits creativity and risk-taking, and denies us the right to shine in front of strangers. And somehow I find that, unaware and without forethought, I have followed Berryman's advice.

When I left my small-town home at 19 to move to San Francisco, I traveled in the direction of my fear and my dreams. College had felt isolating; I wanted real life in the real world, and the city was as strange to me as any foreign land. I had been there only twice, once on a day-long high school field trip, and once for a job interview. When United Airlines offered that job, along with generous passes, I didn't hesitate. For years I had studied maps; now I had a chance to explore them.

And I did. I took advantage of those passes to travel with friends and co-workers. And I took my mother to London, a place she had always longed to see. Later came even more travel with Ray and daughter Jennifer, and now—full circle—I travel again with friends.

And travel has always brought challenges, often with no way out but to acknowledge and deal with them. In ways I could never have dreamt as a child I have had to be brave, to stand up for myself, to find my way. I know now that I am tougher than I look, that I'm capable of withstanding long periods of discomfort and inconvenience.

I can go days and days without even a cold shower, and I can pee into a squat toilet heaped with feces. Dirt no longer deters me, nor does language. I once invited a stranger into a doctor's exam room with me, because he spoke the language and I didn't. I've driven all night while weak from illness while my sick husband lay oblivious in the back seat. I have stolen toilet paper and lied to border guards, and I know how to sacrifice a goat.

There is nothing better I think, than putting yourself in a difficult position and coming out of it whole, and travel is an engaging way to do that. It may even be addictive.

But traveling is about more than conquering fear and overcoming difficulties. We were awed by the beauty we saw, and fascinated by the changing cultures. How could language, customs, habits, food, change so completely at the crossing of an imaginary line? We studied history to understand what we were seeing, tasted unfamiliar foods to better know the people, and said yes! whenever we were invited into someone's home.

We saw that cultures differed by landscape. We watched as the architecture changed from dense northern towns, where houses leaned together for warmth, to the spreading villages of southern Spain and Greece, where thick whitewashed walls kept interiors cool. We experienced the marked differences between east and west; visited grand cathedrals and museums too numerous to count.

And while doing all that we talked with everyone we met. We saw unexpected national characteristics. Germans, for instance, had no problem putting their tent a foot from ours, though the campground was almost empty. We learned that the Dutch always speak English and came to count on them when we were lost.

"Different culture, different customs," we reminded one another through sleepless nights as noisy Australians or Brits drank far more than was good for them. And we watched in delight the voluble Italians and manic Greeks, who went from yelling at one another to hugging without skipping a beat. To our surprise we also learned to love the French, who were quiet campers and always polite and respectful.

But the most important thing I learned was confirmation of something already known. On our deepest level we all want the same things: loving relationships, healthy children, work we enjoy, a life lived in peace.

I came to see the world as a great tapestry and each of us as a single strand in that multi-colored, multi-patterned work of art. I am here, in this turquoise swirl, and others are elsewhere taking part in a geometrical procession or participating in the winding tendrils of a flower. Wherever we stand and however we present ourselves, we are all part of the same masterful pattern. And underneath we are all connected.

I cannot say that every fear is vanquished, for circumstances change and new fears erupt from the shaking ground that is our world. But I am fortunate in this; that in traveling toward my fear, I found myself.

SOVIET UNION–1977

Our trip through the Soviet Union covered 3,812 miles in 39 days, from the Finnish border to the Black Sea, Ukraine, and into Romania. On our own, we were allowed to drive only on specific roads, and we followed a strict and immutable schedule. Police and the KGB knew our route; we were frequently followed.

The cold war was well established. Jimmy Carter was the U.S. President, and Leonid Brezhnev was Communist Party Secretary and head of the Soviet government. The USSR was a failing dictatorship, a poor, sprawling country that had difficulty feeding itself, with an infrastructure that could barely be called that. The contrast between what we saw and knew—that the USSR was a formidable enemy—was a gulf we never managed to cross.

We found it fascinating, troubling, exhausting, amazing, beautiful, and weird.

But it's not the landscapes, the magnificent art,
or the compelling history that make travel worthwhile.
It's the people you meet along the way. Ray knew this
instinctively; he was always ready to visit with anyone we
came across. I had to learn to step out of my comfort
zone to engage with strangers. In the end, however, the
result was the same. We valued the people we met.

The two excerpts below are from Camping With
the Communists *and tell of brief encounters, the first*
untypical (people didn't usually climb walls to talk to us)
and the second a bit of a risk. But like every meeting in
that country these left lasting impressions.

In Piatagorsk

. . . It was later that day that Giorgi climbed over the campground wall and approached the van.

"Hello!" he said, "Do you know anyone in Ohio?"

He was a university student studying English, and unlike most students he had a casual, scruffy look about him. He was, we soon learned, disdainful of his country's government and wanted to emigrate if he could. But he wasn't Jewish—the only legitimate way out at the time. He confessed he had had run-ins with the government and said he didn't care anymore what the officials thought; he would do whatever he wanted. I thought his bravado overblown, but he did have very little hope, and no interest in the political system. "They are all corrupt," he said, and we had to agree.

"But I will leave," he said with determination, after we'd talked for several hours. "I won't live my life here." We were sympathetic, but not optimistic. We hoped he wouldn't end in the gulag.

Giorgi was naturally curious about us and America. He knew a good deal from listening to the VOA and BBC, but many of his beliefs were distorted by the fun-house mirror influence of Soviet propaganda. For instance, he asked me if all the women in America wore décolleté clothing.

When I pointed out that I wasn't wearing a low-cut shirt he replied that might be because of where I was. I disappointed him by laughing at his naiveté, and saying no.

Giorgi was a fount of information about Pyatigorsk and the Caucasus. It was from him we learned that the writer Lermontov had lived and been killed in a duel here. A monument marked the spot, and a small Lermontov museum honored the writer. As a reader and lover of Russian literature I'm surprised I didn't insist on immediately going there. But more important at that moment was Giorgi's willing promise to take us to the outdoor market the following day. He did, and we spent the morning together, continuing our conversation from the day before. The market was a treat. We bought tomatoes, peppers, watermelon, eggs, onions, pears, and cookies. When we separated for the last time, Giorgi asked if we would send him an English dictionary from the U.S.

"Sure, but can we send you other books as well?

"No, just a dictionary. And you must send it to my friend in Ohio, because the police already know I write to her, and it won't get me in more trouble."

We agreed to do so, and before saying goodbye we traded addresses. Not long after we got

back to the U.S. we got a letter from him, direct-
ing us to send things to a friend in Moscow. It was
the beginning of a long, involved relationship.

In Kiev, Ukraine

About 9:30 one evening we were on our way to the campground after a late dinner. We were driving a broad, treelined thoroughfare when we noticed that the bus stops along our route held unusually large numbers of waiting people.

"Have the buses stopped running?" I wondered aloud.

"Maybe they're just late," said Ray. Then he said, "Let's be the bus." At the next stop he pulled the van over and people began climbing in, squeezing themselves onto the bench seat, sitting on laps, and hunching themselves into the space between the back seat and the front, which in our camper van was maybe 18 square feet. We had more people than room.

"Daaaad!" wailed Jennifer, as she scurried over the seat back and found a spot among our sleeping bags.

"It's OK, Jennifer," he said, "they'll be getting out soon." And they did. As we drove the main street our passengers would call out their stops and Ray would pull over and let one or two out. This involved much shuffling of people and belongings but everyone was in a good mood, laughing and commenting on their good luck and the story they would tell when they got home.

But one young couple—Sasha and Tanya—
remained. Sasha had a little bottle of Russian
cognac with him and offered Ray a drink. Tanya
was carrying bundles from her day's shopping,
and insisted I take a couple of pears and a twist of
newsprint. I opened it to find a few tablespoons of
coarsely-ground black pepper, obviously a precious
commodity. I tried to give it back but she refused
to accept it.

Sasha was not drunk but he'd had enough
to feel immune to danger and he was thoroughly
enjoying himself. He "loved Americans" and he
wanted to talk. Tanya was quite nervous, afraid of
being seen by the police, so Jennifer helped them
close the van's side curtains and returned to her
spot behind the seat. We continued through town.
Sasha had a brother who spoke English; he insisted
we go and pick him up. It was impossible to say no
to happy-go-lucky, cheerfully tipsy Sasha, and we
soon found ourselves outside a multistory apartment building. He directed Ray to park in back.

"Lights! Lights!" he yelled as we drove up the
alley. He put his hands to his eyes like binoculars
and Ray quickly doused our headlights.

"Wait here," he said, climbing out of the car.
Tanya stayed with us, and while we waited the two
of us struggled through a meaningless discussion

about nothing in particular. After a wait that felt dangerously long, her husband returned with his brother, a university student named Sergei.

Sergei was adamant that we couldn't park there any longer; it was too risky. So he squeezed in with Sasha and Tanya and we left—very quietly. Ray slowly backed the van from behind the building, our lights out and our voices silent. Thirty minutes later, after making arrangements to meet Sergei at 10 a.m. the next day, we dropped our passengers a few blocks from their home and headed back to the campground, elated by our little adventure, and hoping our new friends wouldn't regret theirs.

PORTLAND

In 1989 we had lived in Eugene for 20 years, and we were ready for a change. Our daughter was through college and on her own. Unable to reach a decision we did what Americans have done since kindergarten; we voted. For 30 days, morning and night, we each dropped a bean into one of three covered jars. The jar labeled Portland won and in January, 1990 we moved there.

We enjoyed the change from town to city and were happy with our decision. During our six years in Portland I worked in the News and Publications office at Reed College. I job shared the last 18 months while writing, with Ray, our first book, How to Plan Your Trip to Europe. *We had been teaching travel workshops and classes and the book began as a brochure of travel tips. It quickly took on a life of its own and we published it in the summer of 1995. Having 3300 books piled in your basement is a great incentive to market and we managed to sell all but a couple of boxes before we left for Turkey in 1996.*

Sunday perch

Summer, 1992

This little balcony is the ideal perch for people watching. The park is quiet this afternoon—no drummers, small children, or dogs about, but plenty of Sunday strollers.

The balcony itself could stand some cleaning. One potted plant, dead or dying, two bicycles, one with a flat tire; two chairs of white plastic, the apartment-dweller's outdoor mainstay; and a nervous orange cat. Oh yes, the fushia plant, purchased today out of Ray's need to acknowledge spring. He misses having a house to putter around in; I love the freedom apartment dwelling brings. Every Sunday we peruse the home section of the newspaper and every Sunday we say again, "it's clear we don't know what we want, let's just stay put awhile longer."

"How long is awhile?" my three-year-old asked many years ago; I still don't have a satisfactory answer. Awhile is a luxury that those of us who trudge daily off to work can't afford. No one has "awhile" anymore, only "now" and "immediately" and "yesterday!"

The homeless man in the red cap is not on his regular bench today. Perhaps he is Madonna-watching with the rest of Portland. He's a proud man, I think, who takes offers of help and proffered food reluctantly. But he likes the children who come from the neighboring nursery school, and I've watched him hold long conversations with the three and four-year olds who bob and weave in front of him as they chatter. I doubt their parents would approve of this friendship, but at least he has lots of awhiles to give.

Lunch-hour interlude

Spring 1994

I'm sitting on the great lawn in front of the college. The day is warm and overcast, though sunlight occasionally dapples the grass. There is a woman in front of the building talking into a microphone, and fragments of her sentences are carried across the lawn to me. She is taking part in a women's "speak out," an exercise meant to promote healing and understanding, and she is talking about being a woman and being abused. I should move closer and listen, but I don't want to.

Instead, I'm reading a book by Virginia Woolf—*Women and Writers*—reading about Jane Austen and Christina Rossetti and George Eliot, while the women's voices go on telling their anger and two male students play soccer in blissful ignorance a few yards away. What a difference between the women of the 18th and 19th century and those of today; the circumspect lives and the outspoken words.

"I should never invite anyone to come and see me who did not ask for the invitation," said George Eliot, but ". . . his hand was through my clothes and on my crotch and I was still in a state of denial," says today's angry young woman.

What would Eliot or Austen think about such words spoken over a loud speaker on a sunny lawn to a mixed crowd of students? Is this progress? I think so, though many don't. The speak-out has been labeled voyeurism by some and male-bashing by others. But when society's guidelines are no longer relevant we must create new ones for ourselves, and isn't it time the rules allowed women their say?

The voices on the lawn fade and strengthen on the breeze while sunlight dances across the green grass. I hear the strident, angry women trying so hard to be heard, to have their issues taken seriously, and I hear the laughing young men concerned only with their game; talking of easy plays and technique.

TURKEY

In early summer of 1996 we moved into an apartment in Gocek, Turkey, as the owners set off on a year-long cruise on their sailboat. They had mentioned their search for renters to our friends in Bodrum, who immediately wrote us. Which is why in 1995 we got a fax in the middle of the night ending with the words, "We think you would like it. Please come."

We had been to Turkey twice and it was a favorite destination. Ray was growing less happy with his job and I was always ready for a change. It wasn't difficult, therefore, to decide to sell our house and car and move to Turkey for a year. Especially since our rent would be only $125 a month.

That year turned out to be, for both of us, "the best year of our lives." How could it not be, with a lovely village to live in, friendly people, beautiful scenery, and much to explore and learn about. I found myself surrounded by the ruins of ancient history, a subject I loved. Ray was able to indulge himself in wandering nearby towns and visiting with strangers, his camera always at the ready. We got around on bikes and buses, occasionally renting a car for a road trip. There was so much to see.

While there I began to email home essays and stories about our life in Turkey. Ray added his own tales, and eventually they became our book, Tea & Bee's Milk: Our Year in a Turkish Village. *The essays that follow offer a taste of our life there.*

Look, listen, live

There's a microwave oven in the tree outside our window. I can't see it, but the beeping sound I hear must mean it's finished cooking and I wish whoever owns it would come and collect it; it's driving me crazy. Maybe it's a bird; it seems to move from tree to tree and I don't think microwave ovens do that. But birds don't sound like that either, do they?

There are other sounds floating through the window this sunny afternoon. The *belediye's* [city hall] red, rusting c.1928 Austin Western grader, the one with the rusting levers, the doorless, almost floorless cab, and the missing windows, is putt-putting somewhere on the other side of the little river. Its engine has a unique pitch so we always know when it's around. One of these days it's going to clank clatter collapse onto its bald-tired wheels and everyone in the village will gather round to mourn, and then they'll carry away the bones and reuse them.

Not far from where the grader is working there's a soccer field, and I can hear the yells and hoots of children kicking a soccer ball around. *Futbol* is the number one sport here, and there's almost always a pickup game going on somewhere in town. This particular field is used every afternoon;

sometimes it's a group from school and there are organized games, other times it's just boys booting a ball.

The noises they make are happy ones though, and I know when I hear them that it's time to stop what I'm doing and think about fixing dinner; or maybe tell Ray to think about fixing dinner.

When the wind is right the sounds of the highway come through the window too. Turks love to toot their horns, which often play more than one note. If I paid closer attention to the various tunes I could no doubt tell you when the *dolmus* passes a certain house, when the Izmir bus goes by the benzene station, and when that friend of the woman who lives on the corner goes to Fethiye. After honking, the most predominant traffic noise is the infamous, high-pitched buzz of motorbikes that pierces glass, clay bricks, and fillings. Their number is legion. We see ancient motorbikes and motorcycles kept running with nothing but baling wire and super glue and appeals to Allah. Nothing mechanical ever seems to be junked here, it gets rebuilt and repainted and repaired and resold and recycled and redeemed.

The *belediye* must be testing new mosquito-killing equipment, for there goes a man carrying something that looks like a leaf blower and roars like only a two-cylinder engine without a muffler can, spitting yards and yards of oily blue smoke and, probably, insecticide. He's following the road next to the river and three boys are chasing along behind, breathing in the fumes and eager to see what's what. Göcek's regular bug machine is an old beat-up pickup with a motor on the back and a big drum filled with something smelly, and it roars down every road in town about once a week during mosquito season. This occasionally causes consternation on the waterfront, as we witnessed one evening last summer. It was a busy Saturday night and the restaurant tables lining the sidewalks and the promenade were full of diners enjoying the balmy evening. Then down the main street, straight through the pedestrians and feet away from scores of diners, comes the bug machine, belching noise and billowing fumes. The tourists grabbed napkins to cover their faces or their food, and a few aimed hard looks at the driver. But this is Turkey after all. Most of us shrugged and kept on eating.

Maybe the warming sun is bringing all these people out; there's a peddler now, calling out his wares. He's the second I've seen in as many days. They've suddenly appeared from nowhere, selling blue, red, and yellow plastic buckets, basins and baskets from off their backs. He pauses for a minute and looks up at the window, but I shake my head no and he turns to saunter back toward the village.

Most of the noises that drift through our afternoon windows are pleasant; the mooing of cows, the clucking of chickens, the pad, pad, swish, swish of grandma's feet moving through the garden below. I like to stay cognizant of grandma's whereabouts (her ever-present cigarette helps), because she has a habit of startling me with incredibly resonant screeches at unexpected moments. Her voice has a high-pitched, glass-breaking tone that would shame a banshee, and when she lets go everyone within a half-mile hears. One of our friends calls these shrieks "barnyard hollers," and says all peasant women develop them to communicate over long distances. I would guess it works.

There's the afternoon prayer call. The *müezzin* sounds stronger now than he did this morning; I was afraid he was coming down with something. I am turning into a regular village busybody, sitting here at the window. But this is one of the things I came to Turkey for—to feel at home with sights and sounds different from those we left behind. And except for the bird that sounds like a microwave oven, I think I'm beginning to succeed.

A Close Shave

Ray writes: As acculturated as I must be after eight months in Türkiye, from time to time I still see things that leave me amazed. Wednesday I drove to Ortaça in Bob and Helen's rental car to pick up a rug for their boat. (To digress, I'm feeling decadent today because for the first time in eight months I drove a car to a store to buy some groceries).

I love going to Ortaça, it's a solid Turkish town of about 15,000 people with few-to-no tourists and little spoken English. The centrum is a tight collection of businesses, near a sizable *otogar* [bus station]. The streets are abuzz with activity; tractors, trucks, motorcycles (some with sidecars), mopeds, cars, mini-buses, big-buses, pushcarts, goats, chickens and people, all going in every direction. Kiosks and vendors abound. I love to walk around, peer into shops, try my taxi Turkish, have lunch, go to the *pazar* and walk the neighborhoods. This is ethnic at ethnic's best.

This day I dropped in on the berber for a shave. Three lads in their early teens led me to the berber chair and directed me to sit and lean my head back on the rest. For the next three minutes I was lathered to an incredible pitch by the young maestro (smartly clad in a white pharmacist's jacket), as his eager and curious assistants looked on. The young berber then honed his straight razor on a wide leather strap, and with the skill of an open-heart surgeon shaved me not once, but twice.

The shave completed, an assistant handed the berber steel forceps that held a cotton ball at their tip. After dipping the cotton in an alcohol solution he ignited it and to my surprise, lightly touched the flaming ball to the inside of each of my ears. Pure genius, I thought, no more scissor cuts removing that nasty, unwanted hair. After the smoke cleared he applied hot steaming towels to my face, covering my eyes, and the massage began. The berber worked on my neck and shoulders as his assistants stepped in to massage my arms and hands. Then came lavish quantities of cologne, followed by aftershave and clouds of talc. A final spray of yet another cologne completed my toilet. Exhausted but unscathed, I paid the berber TL100,000 (80¢) plus a tip, and headed for lunch.

A few doors down from the berber I found a *pide saluno* (four tables and three employees). These are simple restaurants offering a simple menu—*pide*. *Pide* is best described as an elongated, thin pizza with minced meat and parsley spread on top. The sides are folded over, leaving the meat exposed. It's baked in a wood-fired oven, cut into strips and topped with a hunk of butter. Pide is served with hot, dried peppers. Tea and water are available; my coke was brought from a nearby grocery. *Pide* and Coke—TL 200,000 ($1.60).

After lunch I headed for the main street. Waiting to cross, I watched an old car pass slowly in front of me from right to left. A second look confirmed my surprised first impression: from the car's back seat a black cow was gazing forlornly out at me through the rear window. My day was made.

FRANCE

Discovering France was like coming home for both of us. From the first time we set foot there, in 1977, we were lost to its history, its beauty, and its culture. When we left we could hardly wait to return and we did so in 1981, 1987, 1997, and finally in 2000 when in December of that year we purchased a tiny house in a tiny village in the Aude, in southwest France. We were over the moon.

Only 50–60 people lived in the village and we were the only Americans—and we spoke very little French. Nevertheless we were welcomed, invited to fetes and dinners, assisted in our dealings with France's bewildering bureaucracy, and made to feel at home.

The village sat in the crevice of a mountain at the edge of a valley. A spring near the top of that mountain was parent to the noisy, tumbling creek that divided the village and provided water for its gardens and, upstream, a swimming hole. It was crossed by two bridges, one quite ancient. A narrow road paralleled the creek and led

*into a tiny plaza before taking its winding course into the
mountains.*

*The village homes were of stone, generally two
stories. Some, like ours, were remodeled wine caves,
for though wine remained important to the health of the
village, it was no longer the sole source of income. As in
other such villages in the backwaters of France, younger people sought life and work in the bigger towns and
cities, and the village was mostly home to older French
and a few foreigners searching for charm. Most of the
French families had lived there for generations.*

*Ray, an avid cyclist, soon discovered his favorite
routes through the mountains and I found my favorite
walk. I was happy because the narrow roads had few
cars, and because the French drivers were cautious
around cyclers. The changing routes of the Tour de
France always managed to be an easy drive from us
and, much to Ray's delight, we saw five of them before
we sold the house in 2007.*

Hunting Season

December, 2006

Saturday morning had the kind of luxurious air you want to wrap around you—like the softest of pashmina shawls—or pack away in a drawer to bring out again on the darkest winter day. The sun was low and golden in the south, the air humid and warm—it was so beautiful I extended my walk up the hill, going as far as the big bridge before turning around.

Since it was a Saturday, and thus a hunting day, I was a little apprehensive about going too far into the mountains but I saw no *Prudence—Chasse* signs, so kept going. Every Saturday, Sunday, and Wednesday through the fall and winter you will see caravans of little trucks carrying hunters into the hills. Sometimes there are only two or three vehicles; sometimes a dozen or more.

The French hunting style is simple and effective. At their chosen site the hunters park themselves on campstools along the road—well spaced of course—and wait while the hounds are sent down through the brush to scare up a wild boar (*sanglier*). The boar is then herded uphill toward the road where a hunter shoots it. After a successful hunt everyone returns to the starting place and much wine is drunk in celebration.

On hunting days we can often hear the distant barking of the dogs, or the sound of the bells they wear as they roam the hillsides and, of course, the crack of high-powered rifles. I was safely back on the valley floor when the morning's peace was broken by two shots in quick succession. The day turned suddenly dark, the blue and white daisies folded their petals and ducked their heads. The birds ceased singing and the sun hid behind a cloud.

My sympathies are all with the boar. I have been fond of pigs ever since my dad introduced me to piglets on my uncle's farm at the age of four. And though I once munched pork chops with abandon, I always felt guilty about it and gave up the practice long ago. Pigs are special; don't ask me why.

Not surprisingly, my aversion to eating pigs has no influence on the French. Hunting has a long tradition here and it's not likely to end soon despite my wishes or the annual toll in accidents and deaths. A curious tourist was killed this year when she parked near a hunt and got out of the car to watch. Last year a man from our village bled to death when a boar he'd thought was dead gored his leg, slicing the femoral artery. And our local doctor was nearly hit while bicycling this fall, when a bullet hit the ground close enough to spray gravel onto him. The hunter claimed he was "in full control of his shot."

Despite such accidents the hunters are fearless when deciding where to hunt. We often see them within a few yards of busy roads, and coming back from Carcassonne a week ago on the D3 we passed two perched on either side of the highway, guns at the ready. I suppose if a wild boar had charged across the road in front of us, the men would have had no qualms about taking aim and firing. After all, they're in full control.

But even the hunters deserve understanding. Some are poor and the meat supplements their diets. And following good French tradition they use all the pig, not just the prime cuts. I know this, but I am still opposed to hunting.

Unlike me, nature is resilient. Wild boar have lived and been hunted here for thousands of years. (This is, after all, Diana's valley.) Other species have been depleted, if not lost altogether, but the boar remains plentiful enough to be a pest to local gardeners.

By the time all these thoughts had passed through my head the sun had reappeared and the daisies had taken a deep breath and returned to normal. The horses in their pasture wondered why I had forgotten—again!—their carrots, and when I finally stepped through our gate the morning was once again beautiful.

Visitors

July 2006

We haven't had many visitors of the upright, twofooted variety this year, but when a swallow flew in this morning Ray reminded me how many other creatures come to call. It's not unusual to have birds fly through the open street window, circle once or twice, and exit the terrace door. Occasionally a bat will do the same. Sometimes they stay awhile, and when this happens we open all the windows and retreat downstairs. I like birds and bats, but I don't want to share living space with them.

A few days ago Ray moved a scorpion from inside to out and I frightened a snake on the doorstep. We regularly share space with lizards, beetles, giant spiders and little ones, wasps, bees, dragonflies, butterflies, moths, and—my favorite—the Convolvulus Hawkmoth. These look and act like tiny hummingbirds, feeding at the terrace petunias with a four-inch-long proboscis they roll up when not in use. When all this life isn't enough to entertain us we hike up the hill and pet the donkeys, or carry carrots to the several horses in the neighborhood.

Being creatures of the word we often find ourselves talking to our visitors, but unlike the

two-footed kind, these never talk back. They just
flit crawl hop fly, and silently remind us how rich
our environment here is, and how peaceful.

To the Pyrenees

August 2006

We wanted to get out of the village for a few days so we packed up our camping gear and a change of clothes and headed for the Pyrenees. Within an hour we were past Quillan and following the banks of the Aude where it cascades through a rocky, narrow gorge and offers plenty of whitewater for the hundreds of rafters who were either on the river, boarding mini-vans to get on the river, or shaking themselves off after being dunked in the river.

We followed the river through the Gorges de St. Georges and then up and up, over the Port de Pailheres. This is a mountain pass that the Tour de France frequently uses, and the switchbacks are covered with painted names—rider's mostly, but also the names of fans who hope to be seen by the folks back home watching on TV. Parts of this road terrified me, but we made it safely to the foggy top and were welcomed by free-ranging cows and huge friendly horses. Naturally we stopped to pet the horses, and praised the cows for their excellent Pyrenees cheese.

We saw several cyclists along the route and talked with a New Zealander who was riding the Pyrenees from west to east. Some people apparently love to suffer, but as he said, "it's really a drinking trip."

From the top of the pass (2001 meters) we drove down to Ax-les-Thermes—frequently waiting for cows to move off the road—and found a quiet campground on a hill overlooking the town. Unfortunately our campsite was on a slant and I spent most of the night clinging with my fingernails to the cliff of air mattress on my right so that I wouldn't slide down the gully onto Ray. It was also colder than we'd planned for. Neither of us slept well.

The next morning Ray spent an hour talking to a fellow camper—a Dutchman who had nothing good to say about anything. The world was a mess, Lebanon a wreck, Bush a disaster, the weather in Holland awful, the EU incompetent. He'd come to France on holiday but it was too crowded, free camping could no longer be found, and (gasp) the wine was too expensive. (He clearly wasn't buying what we do.) Depression is everywhere.

We spent the morning in Ax, wandering through curving streets and munching on patisserie goodies. Ax is primarily a ski center and we wanted to take the gondola to the top, but alas, it was *ferme*. Since we were both exhausted from lack of sleep we decided to look for a new, flat campsite that was lower down the mountain and thus, we hoped, warmer.

We found it in the little village of Roque-feuil, in a campground that had been open only a month. This was by far the cleanest site we've stayed in. The showers were tiled and polished, with ample hot water. The lawns were mowed and divided by hedges into plots. The lighting was limited and subdued. It was uncrowded and it was flat. Heaven!

Somehow we failed to note that it was next door to the village church. In France the church bells always ring twice so that, presumably, if the farmer in the field misses it the first time, or only hears part of it, he will pay attention the second time. The fact that farmers now wear watches or carry iPhones has no bearing on French tradition, which is unchanging and sacrosanct. From 10 p.m. until morning we heard the bell count the hour 68 times (including one stroke every half-hour). And it rained. It began as a light mist about 10 p.m., then pelted down all night. The next morning we packed up our tent and all our belongings in the rain and headed home.

In the Val de Dagne

April 2007

The field is many shades of green, but brush-strokes of gold and white spread across and down the canvas, accentuating the gentle hill that stretches before me.

It is that touch of color that is my delight every year at this time, for it's wildflower season in the Val de Dagne and the show is just beginning. Yellow and white lead the way, but each day on my walk I see new colors, some vivid, some pale. Today tiny blue, and light purple blossoms appeared, along with the showy red poppies that keep shouting, "Me! Me! Me!" Last year I counted over 50 varieties on one walk. This year we'll be leaving the valley before so many reveal themselves. *C'est la vie.*

Every year I expect to see someone with an easel and a paintbrush setting up beside the road, and every year I'm disappointed. Photographs are fine, but this delicacy requires a painter. Maybe this will be the year some discouraged Montmartre Monet will lose his way on the road to Barcelona and discover that his heart and talent were destined to record this scene. I can think of no better way to spend one's time.

I heard a new bird in Villar this afternoon. It was unlike any I've heard before, its call like the clear, sharp sounding of a perfectly formed small brass bell. Ding, ding, ding, ding, pause one two three; ding, ding, ding, ding, pause one two three; ding, ding, ding, ding. . . .

Maybe it wasn't a bird at all. Maybe it was just what it sounded like, a tiny bell tolling in the field-elves and fairies for their daily reporting. It could be, you know. Magic still happens here.

Hail!

April, 2007

It woke us about midnight, clattering on the clay-tiled roof upstairs. Pulled from a dream, I thought someone was knocking on the door.

"Hail," said Ray, in what was soon revealed as understatement.

We lay listening as it progressed from clattering to crashing to banging with sledgehammers. We tentatively climbed the stairs, the racket increasing with every step. Surely, the skylight would shatter under the barrage. It was like being inside a machine gun. Lightning flashed continually, adding its rumble and boom to the surround-sound effects.

Streetlights revealed a landscape thickly covered with large frozen pellets. Leaves and twigs were sliced from branches. Madame's newly-planted pansies and petunias lay pulverized in their pots. Our patio was littered with leaves, dirt, and bamboo from the overhead shade. The hedge, praised that morning for its bountiful new growth, was shredded.

The noise stopped ten minutes later, the lightning passed on to the north, and after checking the car windows (all fine) we went back to bed. Life in rural France is nothing but excitement.

Monmouth

After leaving France we settled in Monmouth, a small town that was home to Western Oregon University. It was a compromise, half way between Portland, where our daughter and her family lived, and Eugene/Corvallis where most of our friends were. It wasn't France, but we tried to love it.

I finally had the time and space to finish and publish Tea & Bee's Milk. *Print-on-demand had arrived so there was no need for stacks of book boxes in the garage. I continued to walk daily, joined a writing group, and met my new neighbors.*

Some of Ray's efforts still reverberate, like the Google group he started for the neighborhood, along with an annual clean-up day. He worked on noise and light issues, and convinced his bike club to celebrate a local man who had ridden a between-cities bike path for years, eventually logging 10,000 miles. When the state wouldn't put up a sign, Ray did it for them.

Saying farewell to France had been a wrench and I suspect that any place we chose after that would eventually have been rejected. And though we loved our house, and had good friends in Monmouth, we never felt at home. In 2011, after a year on the market, the house finally sold, and once again we packed everything and prepared to move.

My red dog day

January 2008

We've been having lots of rain and cold here and when I head out on my morning walk I'm usually bundled to the max. I don't know who invented fleece but they have my heart.

A couple of days ago I was trudging up the sidewalk, wrapped in layers of fleece and pretty much oblivious to my surroundings. I was in this semi-somnolent state when a young dog came tearing up beside me. A hound of some kind, reddish brown and in a high state of ecstasy, as though he'd finally found freedom after months in a dark kennel. He was running fast and hugging the ground, and his long legs stretched forward and back so far that he looked like a fold-up toy.

His happiness was taking him in long joyful loops, his nails clicking loudly on the pavement. I was crossing the street when he headed straight for me. I had no time to react and was lucky he didn't knock me down when he leapt up and tried to lick my face. His claws dug into my leg and I was grateful for the layers of fleece. He took off again and ran straight into the street where he just missed being hit by the rear tire of a large, fierce-looking truck.

The driver stopped and the passenger-side
window slid slowly down. I knew he was going to
yell, "Why don't you keep that damned dog on a
leash?" so before he had a chance I shrugged my
shoulders, held out my arms and said, "I don't
know who that dog belongs to."

And the driver smiled and said, "Are you all
right?"

The universe keeps sending me this lesson and
I keep forgetting it. "Don't assume. Don't assume.
Don't assume."

Desert stillness

September, 2008

After feeling compelled to watch both political conventions we could think of nothing more healing than a trip to the Oregon desert. We shoved our new five-day cooler into the car's back seat, added groceries, tent, bedding, and a couple of changes of clothes, and were out of town by 9 a.m. Monday morning. At 5:30 we were unfolding shock poles in a remote, quiet campground in empty Harney County. Except for a group of state workers camped at the end of the road, we had the place to ourselves.

The stillness was acute. We might have been in the crosshairs of David Bohm's implicate-explicate order—the nothing from which all arises. The air was still and dry. Nothing moved. No chipmunks scurried about waiting to raid our camp. No jays hollered at us from the trees. Only insects kept us company for three days of blissful quiet. In the mornings we were visited by grasshoppers, in the afternoons, flies; in the evenings, moths—and bats.

We hiked a little, we read, we ate; we tried to play petanque but the ground was too rocky. We explored the campground and the horse camp nearby. We built campfires and watched the moon grow from 40 percent to almost full. We walked the campground road by that light, in awe of the moon shadows. We heard coyotes howl in the distance. But most of the time we sat reading, our chairs at opposite ends of camp, soaking up the absence of all sound. It was utterly restful.

On the fourth day we drove west again, as far as the Metolius River where we camped for two more days. Weekend campers arrived Friday night; their hustle and noise preparing us for the inevitable return to civilization. We arrived home late Saturday, weary and dusty, but renewed.

On a rainy Easter

April 2010

A plump male pheasant is striding elegantly through the field beside our house. He keeps ruffling his red and green and chocolate-brown feathers; shedding the rain maybe, or just showing off. He's a colorful addition to the landscape this Easter day, but it's a good thing no hunting is allowed. His bright white neck ring is a can't-miss bulls eye against the spreading green field.

Easter is just another day for us—except for the small excitement generated by the Easter bunny's visit to our granddaughter. But it's a day that always causes me to reconsider my own beliefs. In some ways changed, in other ways remarkably consistent since childhood, when regular church going was part of the routine and Easter meant music and familiar faces, and the chance to wear a new dress and patent leather shoes.

The last Easter service I remember attending was in the early 70s. As Ray and I took our seats in the Unitarian sanctuary the stranger next to me leaned over and asked, "Well, do you believe?"

"Believe what?" I asked

"That Jesus rose from the dead."

"I don't know."

"I don't know either," he said, "but I'd like to think He did."

Risking heresy, I think we should be paying far more attention to the message and far less to the death of the messenger.

The pheasant in the field has no thoughts about the risen or not-risen Christ on this day, and yet the pheasant is beautiful and whole and perfect and content to be what he is. No organized religion is clambering for his attention or chastising him for his sins (what an old-fashioned word) or governing his morals. He and the stalking cat and the blowing daffodils are free to follow their path in whatever way they wish.

I think we all have that option.

Will science become religion?

Religion is a topic I'm interested in as an observer rather than a participant, but it's one that increasingly consumes our public discourse. I don't believe it belongs in the political realm, but it seems to have grown roots there and its influence is inescapable.

For instance, on Monday the new governor of Alabama, Robert Bentley, speaking to a group gathered to honor Martin Luther King day, stated: "So anybody here today who has not accepted Jesus Christ as their savior, I'm telling you, you're not my brother and you're not my sister, and I want to be your brother." I found this highly offensive coming from someone who had been elected to represent the thousands of unique individuals in Alabama, and I wondered how Dr. King—or Jesus—would respond.

Maybe this comment struck a nerve because the previous day we had watched "Baraka," a 1992 film that begins and ends with images of religious worship throughout the world. The film has no narration and the images are left for us to decipher on our own, to make what we will of the creative and colorful ways humans seek meaning in our world. It was the religious creativity that impressed me most, and without the unspoken dogma and the muted and irrelevant rules, I was ready to go along with any of them. ("Baraka" also speaks to the damage we've inflicted, but that's a topic for another time.)

There are those who believe the universe itself is a continuing act of creation, set in motion by an unseen hand or force and participated in by every living thing. I like this idea, and it was given credence in an interview we heard Sunday evening on Krista Tippett's radio show, *On Being*. Tippett interviewed physicist and Anglican priest Dr. John C. Polkinghorne about the ideas in his book, *Quarks, Chaos, & Christianity*. Science now accepts that on a quantum level the observer influences the outcome, and the deeper and more quantum the science goes, the more convincing becomes the fact that we are the creators of our reality.

But these ideas aren't religion yet, and probably won't be in my lifetime. Still, I prefer believing that we all participate in, and have a responsibility for, creating a peaceful, more perfect world. Meanwhile, I'll try to be tolerant of Robert Bentley's exclusionary beliefs. They are, after all, just another point of view.

COSTA RICA

While waiting for our house to be built in Sisters, Oregon we searched around for an inexpensive place to go and settled on Costa Rica. Because it was late in the year we had trouble finding a rental that wasn't booked for the holidays. Eventually we found a little flat in Manuel Antonio where we spent ten weeks. It wasn't ideal but it was affordable and after a few weeks it didn't matter: we caught a circulating, debilitating bug that kept both of us ill, coughing, and without energy for most of our stay.

Living with life

November 2011

Our landlord Rodney came over this morning, bringing with him a bottle of poison for the large ants trying to take over our bathroom. They were building a nest at the bottom of the wooden sink cabinet and for the last three mornings I've swept up little piles of debris they had created overnight. The ants were no problem, but the sweeping was getting old. Rodney sprayed, wiped it down, and went home; but the ants, once limited to life in the bathroom, now scurry in ones and twos over the main room's tiled floor, escaping from the poison no doubt. We leave the door open so they can find their way out.

While Rodney was here he also sprayed around the kitchen window to keep the fire ants at bay. They are the smallest ants we've ever seen, light brown in color and so tiny they can easily be overlooked. They bite though, and leave a power-ful stinging behind that lasts a good 30 minutes. We have no compunction about killing them.

Yesterday, in the drawer where we keep the wires and chargers that modern travel demands, I found a large brown beetle, a good inch long, not counting his feelers. He was dead so we didn't have to chase him down to carry him out, which is a good thing. I felt bad though—I like beetles.

There are other insects of course; mosquitoes have shown their ugly little snouts now that the rains are passing, and moths and other winged insects occasionally pass through (our rear windows have no screens). And of course, like every tropical household we have a gecko. He's small and doesn't get in our way, but it's a little disconcerting sometimes to reach for a package or can and see him dodging away across the kitchen counter.

Fortunately neither of us is especially squeamish about insects or creepy crawlers, and living surrounded by jungle I guess that's a good thing. Still, I much prefer the monkeys; they're a lot more fun.

The unwelcome guest

November 2011

When I pulled out the wireless keyboard this morning I was surprised to find it wasn't working. The space bar wouldn't space, the r, y, h and i keys wouldn't r, y, h, or i. The caps lock INSISTED on capping. Uh oh.

A quick search on the Apple site brought us the obvious answer: humidity over 80 percent may affect this device. There's no hint whether the humidity saps the keyboard's energy as it does ours or whether mold simply overtakes its innards; regardless, it has been sent to dry out, like a recovering alcoholic.

Living in the Willamette Valley for 40 years means we're no strangers to occasional mold and mildew but it reaches an entirely new level here in the rain forest. Not long ago we found Ray's shoelaces suddenly sprouting blue hair; then my canvas shoes came out of the closet covered in gray. Looking further we discovered the backpack exhibiting a patina of new life and—oh crap—there it was again on a polyester satchel. I like to think I love life in all its permutations but this form is definitely unwelcome.

It's impossible to keep things completely dry when humidity hovers at 85–90 percent so we resort to making sure the heavy air circulates as much as possible. Closet and cupboard doors and drawers are left ajar, damp towels and sweaty shirts are immediately carried outside to be pegged to the line, and shoes are no longer kept in the closet but are parked around the room's periphery. The overhead fan runs 24/7 and we keep a wary eye out for new intrusions.

For a confessed neatnik these are tough adjustments, and I struggle to ignore the chaos. Humidity, I tell myself, is good for aging skin, and it's obviously loved by the local flora. If I'm not covered with gray fuzz when we leave here, maybe I'll look like a flower.

Pura vida

January 2012

A column in today's *New York Times,* "The Joy of Quiet" by Pico Iyer, reminded me that our intention in coming to Costa Rica was to enjoy a few months of quiet. We have not found that, though it seems unimportant now; we have grown accustomed to the daily sounds surrounding us. Iyer's focus is about saving silence and quiet time for children, but all of us who depend on the Internet and electronic devices already know we are losing something inestimable.

We rely heavily on the Internet here, for communication, news, and entertainment. Ray uses a laptop and I use my iPad. An iPod is plugged into portable speakers through which we hear music and podcasts. Our photographs reach the world in a few seconds. This is all good and helpful in its way. But it is a far cry from true silence, a gift that was with humans from our beginning and should be still. Now we are lucky if we recognize scattered moments.

"Listen!"

"To what?"

"Nothing."

Because our house is right next to a worn and pot-holed road and a speed bump, we hear, not cars and trucks driving smoothly past, but cars and trucks braking, driving through a gravel patch to avoid the bump, and bouncing over the bump. We hear the merchandise headed to the little living-room grocery down the road slamming and bouncing in the truck beds (the trucks are nearly as big as the shop). We hear souped-up cars scraping bottom on the bump and motorcycles accelerating across it.

Other daily sounds include the footsteps of our upstairs neighbors, the crying of the teething baby next door, the voices of conversations and calls up and down the street, pounding rain, barking dogs, the occasional singing of Dago, our neighbor, and when we're lucky, bird calls. In the depths my illness I slept through it all and now it's part of my life and seldom noticed. It's also part of the culture we came to explore and thus is easier to accept. (Different culture, different customs.)

As a writer, I've always found describing sound a difficult chore. Onomatopoeia, words that suggest the sound they describe (cackle, boom, tinkle) do good work but they lack a crucial element: the effect noise has on the human body. For we hear not only with our ears. Our entire body reacts when a truck bounces over a speed bump 20 feet away, or a firecracker goes off unexpectedly outside the window. Our heart pounds, our nervous system twangs, our brain orders a shot of adrenalin. Even when we don't acknowledge the sound, don't hear it out of custom, our body hears it and filters it and reacts to it. Sometimes it replays, altered, in dreams. That's hard to capture in one short sentence.

Fortunately, firecrackers don't often explode outside our windows, but the constant drone of ever present noise, even when it comes from You-Tube or an iPod, has a wearing effect on the body. Finding silence is one of the best things you can do for yourself, and though we misjudged its presence here, we'll never stop pursuing it. Maybe we'll find it next year.

Later: We had a bit of excitement this afternoon when we heard a new and surprising noise. Three motorcycle policeman chased a wayward driver down our road, sirens blaring. Naturally we went out to look so we were handy when Daniel, one of the officers, came over to ask for two glasses of water, please. We watched as the car was moved and searched and we waited while the young officers stood around and flirted with young women passing by. Finally the traffic truck came and issued a ticket—or something—and Daniel returned our glasses and the excitement was over.

Before he left Daniel put an arm around each of us and speaking in broken English said very seriously, "Life is good. And the world is small."

Pura vida is difficult to translate; the closest is "plenty of life." You see it everywhere here, on tee shirts, caps, paintings and pottery. People have said it to me on the street, always accompanied by a big smile. It's used to express many things but I like to think it's what Daniel was trying to say. Life is good, and we're all in it together. *Pura vida!*

Leaving on a jet plane

February 2012

We arrived in Portland late Sunday, and three loads of laundry later it feels as though our ten weeks in Manuel Antonio never happened. Only the photographs make it real, and already we are caught in the ongoing busyness of life in Norteamericana.

It is quiet here compared to our little MA apartment. There are chickens but no roosters and traffic on this street is almost nil. Neighbors are not hollering at neighbors, trucks and motorbikes are not bouncing across a speed bump, and no one is plucking a chicken in the back yard. There is a fat cat here, but no monkeys.

The problem with traveling is that you have to go home, a difficult prospect for confirmed travelers even when the travel has been less than exciting. Coming home is hard. All this damn mail to deal with—and thank goodness Ray doesn't seem to mind. All these people to contact, all these errands needing to be run. All this laundry and unpacking and sorting and putting. Give me a plane or a bus or a train or a camel to anywhere, and take me away from all these musts and shoulds.

Maybe what I'm feeling is simply culture shock. Air travel is entirely too fast and the in-air experience, once romantic and exciting, is now a miserable timelessness that extends to a horrible infinity with breaks for crackers and soft drinks. Destinations, whether home or an exotic port, should be approached slowly—preferably on foot—so that one can observe and absorb the gradations of the landscape and the subtly shifting cultural patterns. One should ease into a place, not be dropped into it with cold, high tech abandon. Next time I'm taking a slow freighter. Or maybe I just need a good night's sleep.

Sisters, Oregon

We arrived in Sisters in March, 2012, hoping it would be our last move. The small community quickly felt like home and we were pleased we'd made the change. It wasn't France, but it was good, and the nearby mountains and pine forests meant the natural world and its beauty were close at hand. Ray quickly added to his list of cycling challenges by regularly riding the route from Sisters to McKenzie pass, a climb of 2129 feet in 13 miles. I settled into my own routine, a daily three-mile walk past the tall ponderosa pines which inspired many of these pieces.

We rock

June 2012

It's gray here today but after several days of hard rain we're assured that at least of week of sunshine and temps in the high 70s are on the way. I find the gray depressing and since we moved here for the sun I'm a little put out that we're having an "unusual" wet spring. "Be equanimous" declared a friend's yoga teacher, and I try, I try. I find equanimity a lot easier, however, when the sun shines.

A slew of company passed through a few weeks ago, four sets in fewer than three weeks. The company and the yard have kept us busy, and kept me away from the writing I promised myself. But you must agree that having an empty dirt lot out the back door requires urgent action. And since we're doing the work ourselves, urgent action equals time consumed—it's not an excuse. Since this is desert country we're creating a xeriscape (low-water) yard with lots of native plants and rocks, including a dry creek that will emerge from the not-yet-built deck and disappear under the far fence.

As a result of our need I've become rock enthralled; I see them everywhere. "Getting rocks" has become one of my favorite things to do, but I find it curious that even though we need thousands

I still pick and choose as I pick them up. Why I pass over some and grasp at others—with little visible difference between them—is a mystery.

The garden's future plants are no mystery, they are easily purchased at a nearby nursery. The rocks, however, require a lot of lifting and carrying, and that's after we've picked them off the ground and hauled them home. Yesterday each of us must have carried several hundred pounds that we'd picked up in the field where developers dump their land-clearing trash. It's a treasure trove of stones of all sizes and shapes, mostly volcanic.

Here in the West volcanic activity marks most of our history. The Native Americans were too smart to build monuments to themselves or their civilizations, and the rest of us began arriving only 200 years ago (Fort Astoria, the first Oregon settlement, was built in 1811). This is the equivalent of less than a blink in the evolutionary timescale.

As a fan of history I loved the grand and ancient ruins of Turkey and the prehistoric caves of France. It was comforting to be surrounded by these visible signs of our continuing. Here, where the wooden structures of pioneer towns are already disintegrating, I rely on the nearby mountains for that sense of continuity. It is different, of course, for mountains go on with or without us, yet the spirit—and comfort—I receive from their presence feels the same. The volcanic rocks we carry home, and dig out of our own plot of dirt, are long on continuity. They will be here after we and our culture are sunk and forgotten.

Many years ago I read an anecdote from poet and writer Gary Snyder that I've always loved.

> "One night, when he [Welch] was still alive he was sitting with me by a campfire…& after a long while of silence, he said to me, "Gary, do you think the rocks pay attention to the trees?" and I said, "Why, I don't know Lew. What are you driving at?" and he said, "Well, the trees are just passing through."

It's curious

February 2013

It had been almost a year since we'd set foot on Willamette Valley clay, and we were curious to see what had changed. It's very odd that here in Sisters I seldom think of the valley, our home for almost 40 years, and when I do it seems far, far away. In fact, it's only a two-and-a-half-hour drive.

We had promised to visit friends we had known in other lives, people we felt the need to touch again. But our sudden decision to go now meant we missed some of those we'd set out to see. One was on her way to Australia, another had the flu and a third had moved to Salem. So we dutifully drove to Salem and had a good visit with our former neighbor, a strong and healthy woman of 87. Emily was always active, in politics, on boards, and as a volunteer. Ray and I managed her first campaign for city councilor in 1978 (she won) and talking with her again felt much the same. Yes, she's slowed a little but her voice is strong, she still perches on the edge of her seat, ready to leap to the fray; still tilts her head, birdlike, when she talks. She's active, still driving, still curious.

In Tangent we enjoyed a stay with good friends Jo and Seaton. Jo's mother Trudi lives in what our English friends would call a bed-sit attached to their home. Trudi is 95, and like Emily she still drives, still attends book club, occasionally swims, loves to read and enjoys her family.

From Tangent to Portland, where we stayed with our daughter and family for a few nights, and visited 79-year-old Marianne. Marianne is the liveliest of the three, flitting between three homes (one in France) and various grandchildren who always seem to be celebrating milestone events. Her travel schedule for this year rivals that of many diplomats. Next May she'll be taking 19 family members to Costa Rica to celebrate her 80th birthday. She confessed that she is thinking of selling the French house "in five years." This made us sad because we love her French house. But her unabashed optimism made us happy.

Thinking about these aging-well women— and about the one who had flu and is 82 and still attends board meetings and arranges events and makes everyone snap to attention—I realized that, though living disparate lives they have much in common. All are strong, independent-minded women who cared deeply about the work— paid and unpaid—that filled their days. All have well-funded retirements and family who can be counted on. And all retain their curiosity, a trait that opens our hearts and minds to the world, with all its glories and despite its shortcomings.

It is this characteristic I find most interesting for I seldom hear it mentioned in discussions of aging. We all know curiosity drives invention but it also pushes us, and teaches. It is a trait that can keep us going when our bodies are too tired to move, requiring only a bit of concentration and a willingness to open a book or tap on a keyboard to explore the universe.

I confess I have little patience with the incurious, but some sympathy too. It takes guts to move beyond the confines of one's beliefs; it can be scary out there. But my guess is that curiosity is a powerful motivator that keeps at least some of us living beyond our allotted years.

From now to a memory

March 2013

I stumbled on a TED talk about memory this morning and since that's a subject I'm keenly tuned to, having lost family and friends to Alzheimer's, I watched. Joshua Foer's talk is about competitive memorizing—who knew?—and he shows us some of the tricks competitors use. But the heart of his talk is this, that you must work to remember. And you must pay attention to the present. I latched onto that because it's what I believe too, and we're always ready to adopt an expert when he agrees with us. But in this case my experiences support my belief.

We've done a lot of traveling through the years and have been rewarded with wonderful memories. Most remain bright and clear because when you travel as we did, with little money and almost always by car you must, if you are to keep going, pay attention to the present. If you're on the road in a foreign land, following road signs you can't read, eating foods you don't know, struggling through a conversation in mutually unintelligible languages, and seeing strange and beautiful things every minute of every day, you can't help but be present and alert. Otherwise, to quote recently deceased author Chinua Achebe, "things fall apart."

Some of the sites and some of the conversations we had during those travels are burned into my soul. It is day-to-day living that depletes our memories, it is the deep ruts we carve for ourselves and the mundane activities that fill our lives: eating, bathing, cleaning, working, shopping, commuting. Not to mention all the electronic distractions. Yet even in this we find relief when we pay attention.

On my routine daily walks I am often so deep in my mind that I only surface when I'm about to be hit by a car. Most days I cannot tell you what I saw or heard. But when we pay attention, memory works. A few weeks ago I was obliviously walking the asphalt path when a sudden movement on the left caught my eye. I turned to see eight deer, the nearest standing less than ten feet away. I had already passed most of them and would have missed them entirely except for that nod of the head. Of course I stopped and greeted the ladies—they were all ladies—and we stood and looked at each other. Then, not wanting to spook them I moved on.

On another day Ray and I were walking when I looked up and saw two large birds circling high above us. "Look," I said, "are those vultures?" And as I spoke one of the great birds turned toward us and the morning sun lit up his white head and tail feathers. We watched as the bald eagle circled lower and lower on a descending current of air. Then suddenly he flapped his wings and was off again, disappearing over the tops of the pines. I remember that, just as I remember the deer, because they were events that drew me out of my routine and into the present.

Distractions like those are frequent here and we are lucky, but anyone can be aware. I sometimes pretend I'm on a trip just to practice the awareness that I know goes with traveling. It's not hard, it just takes remembering to do it.

Give yourself a present today. Step out of your routine for just a moment and notice your surroundings; pay attention. Don't, as Foer says, "be so lazy that [you're] not willing to process deeply." Look hard. Your present is your present, and it can be a memory.

Being a tree

April 2013

Today I shared my walk with a steady downpour of small ice pellets. The hail was nothing to me, I barely felt it, but for three miles I watched it hit the pavement, bounce or roll, and disappear into waiting pools of water or the black heat of the asphalt path itself. I looked up at the clouds and tried to estimate how long a lifespan those pellets had—how long had it taken them to drop from the cloud to the ground. A minute maybe? Two at most. A short lifespan, but I'm sure they were the best ice pellets they could be during their lifetime. They had nothing to be ashamed of.

I looked too at the tall pine trees and wondered if this quickly shifting spring weather, from sunny and 70 to 23 and snowing, was hard on them. Did they wish, like me, that the weather would settle down and just be something—anything? No, that's anthropomorphizing, and though I do it all the time I didn't want to think of the trees that way. They're too majestic to be treated as mere mortals.

Unlike us humans, who trot off busily to whatever distraction occupies us, the trees stand still. They are as permanent as a living thing can be. Trees can't hitch up their boughs and run away on their scraggly roots. They're stuck with whatever comes: sun, snow, wind, hail, lightning, locusts, fire. The trees take it. They suck it up. They stand there through whatever lifespan they're given and are the best tree they can be. Trees are the essence of being.

It would surely serve us if we could be more treelike. If we could think of ourselves less as busy, successful, coping human doings and more—just occasionally—as human beings. If we could just stop. And be. Occasionally. Just be.

Saying hello to silence

July 2013

When I left the house this morning I was enveloped by silence. The early morning air was still cool and few people were about. The silence is welcome and, as I'm sure I've said before, it's one of the things I like best about living here. I hear only my footsteps on the path, the scrape of a stone on my shoe.

A woman walking two dogs crosses in front of me at the corner, and I think she must be training the younger one, for I repeatedly hear "heel! heel" and constant clucking, as though she were urging on a horse. I'm happy when she continues up the opposite side of the road, and now I can hear the twittering of unseen birds and the sweet call of a dove.

Despite the busyness of the summer season and the influx of tourists, it's still possible to find silence here, and I think of all those living in cities who must forego this luxury. I like cities myself, I enjoy the busyness, the sense of doing and accomplishment that goes with the hum and squawk of traffic and the sound of many feet hitting the pavement. Even when you have nothing of importance to do, being surrounded by all that hustle can make you feel that your nothing has value. Even so, I'm glad I no longer live in a city.

As my walk grows in length and the hour gets later, more traffic appears. Early-service church goers pull into parking lots, tourists in overstuffed cars head up the pass, and cyclists breeze past on their way to the mountain's challenge. Silence gives way to daily life. I meet two other walkers, neither of whom speaks when I offer my casual "g-morning." I mark them down as tourists, for locals, even when strangers, inevitably speak; sometimes even stopping to comment on the weather or some other mutually satisfying event. It's the advantage of a small town, and I like it.

It was also one of the things I liked about living in France; unless you were in the midst of a crowd, everyone said "bon jour" or "bon soir" when you crossed paths. I missed it on our return and decided I would carry on the tradition.

A few weeks ago I came up behind an older man slowly walking a bicycle. He was clearly a vagabond, but clean and neatly dressed. He wore a blue backpack on which he had scrawled, in bold white lettering, "Danger. Do Not Talk to Me!" followed by a skull and crossbones.

I read those words and without giving it much thought decided that a "good morning" didn't count as talk. So when I passed him I spoke. I was surprised to hear him reply with a cheerful

"Good morning" and then, "Beautiful day isn't it?" I turned and raised my arms. "Gorgeous," I declared.

And then I turned back and walked on, wondering what it was about talk that he didn't like. Maybe he just prefers the ringing in his ears to the empty chatter of others. Or maybe, like me, he just can't get enough of silence.

It's about science—or not

February 2014

It hasn't snowed for days here in Sisters country, and the asphalt paths are finally clear of ice. It was a relief this morning to walk on solid ground instead of skipping from dry spot to dry spot over ice and snow. There are, however, mounds of dirty snow everywhere, melting in odd, disproportionate ways. I suddenly realized I was seeing poorly carved snow sculptures in the melting piles. It was like finding familiar figures in cloud formations, and within a quarter-mile stretch I spotted a goose, two horses fighting, a lopsided crown, and a carefully balanced butterfly. None were perfect. As with clouds, they required imagination.

Science would no doubt affirm that sun and wind had carved the fantastical shapes, but this morning I preferred a different solution. The sculptures had, I was sure, been carved by fairies wielding swords that were too heavy for them. I could see them in my mind's eye. They were trying, poor dears, to embellish the dirt-covered snow with objects of beauty, but clearly they needed better tools.

I'm not discounting science. I'm more apt to see evolution in nature than fantasy, but I always leave room for the latter. I resist the dominance of materialism* whenever I can, and if Eileen Cady, of Findhorn fame, chooses to tell me that Pan gave her the advice she needed to grow huge cauliflowers in North Scotland sand, then I will choose to believe her. Because why not?

I do love science though, and often find myself struggling through tomes I barely understand, in order to better comprehend my world. But science, especially physics, is now as magical as a medieval necromancer. Some physicists tell us that string theory works if there are eleven dimensions instead of four; but don't ask to see those dimensions because they're much too tiny and curled within themselves. So on days like this I say, okay then, fairies and gnomes and ghosts and tree sprites and Sasquatch do exist. They just retreat to one of those invisible dimensions when humans appear. Can you prove me wrong?

---

*My dictionary states that "materialism is the doctrine that nothing exists except matter and its movements and modifications"; a grim kind of philosophy in my book. Read that sentence again, replacing the word *matter* with *money*, and you have a picture of 21st century America.

On break at a writing conference

Summer 2014

The little creek burbles and bubbles over a low rock dam. In the calm green water behind are native grasses and what I think are Iris, not yet blooming.

The heat of the morning sun warms my feet, which are damp from the dew still lingering on the grass. The drops gleam like silver, but one, directly in the sun's path, is solid gold. A bird twitters, and in the background a garbage truck crashes and bangs, temporarily destroying the peace of the morning.

I love the carefully placed rocks, for they are carefully placed despite the natural look of the area. I wish I had some of these rocks in my yard, like the large flat one I'm sitting on. I consider the consciousness of rocks and wonder if this one cares that I am resting my bum on it.

To be rock. Silent, impassive, aware but uncaring. Living deep, deep down and away from the surface of a human's busy life, as though asleep, or half asleep. Watching the world fly by while sitting ageless. Loving the feeling of unmoving permanence. Contributing one's weight to the service of a stream, a bum, a bird. Solid, timeless, and content.

While sitting beside the Metolius River

Summer, 2014

If all things have consciousness—and scientists and sages seem to be drawing closer on this—if all things have consciousness does the water know its value? Its place in the world? Its destination?

Does the ocean heave and breathe and sigh with sadness as it watches the coral die, the water turn acidic, the fish and mammals moving but still dying? Does the ocean speak to the planet? Does it understand the warming?

Do the trees talk with the water? Does everything but us understand the planet suffers and may die?

Such a beautiful world. Such a beautiful river. Hear the gurgling, cascading, roaring water and give thanks.

The cabin

July 2014

The cabin sits halfway along a narrow gravel road that dead ends a mile or so farther on. It's a small structure, a single room with a couple of closet-sized bedrooms for the children and an attic room accessed by a narrow ladder, where the adults sleep. There are two propane stoves for heat and a charming 1920s propane cook stove in the kitchen alcove. In the evenings the woman lights the hanging gas lanterns, and sometimes oil lamps.

Behind the house, a few steps off the covered back porch and about ten feet away, depending on the season, is a busy creek. It tumbles over boulders and rocks and in summer it sends out an agreeable burbling sound, a baseline for life in the cabin. In winter, when the water is high, the creek roars, even when muffled by snow.

Surrounding the cabin and the creek are old-growth Douglas firs. The trees grow tall on massive trunks that spread heavy branches in search of sunlight. They loom over the little cabin and dominate the view. There are other trees though, downed by wind or lightning, or simply old age. They lie canted across the landscape in various stages of decay. The older ones are nurse trees, their rot providing sustenance for ferns and flowers, and eventually other trees. Branches, limbs, twigs, lay where they fell. The forest understory is dense with ferns, huckleberry, deer brush, Oregon grape, vine maples, salmonberry, mushrooms and numerous wild flowers.

The first time I saw an old growth forest I was disappointed. It looked messy. I immediately wanted to start dragging away the downed branches and raking up debris. I wanted neatness and spare undergrowth so I could see the trees in all their glory. But then I understood. This is their glory.

This forest and the little cabins scattered along the creek are here because in 1910 the Star Brewing company in Portland received permission from the U. S. Forest Service to construct a hotel and resort near a mineral spring.

The 70 room hotel offered flower gardens, a dance pavilion, horseback riding, and mineral baths. Only an hour and a half from Portland and Vancouver, the land deep in the Gifford Pinchot forest offered a peaceful respite to busy city dwellers. And because forest plans of the early 20th century required buffer zones around roads and establishments like the hotel, the surrounding forests were protected from logging. The trees, the creek, and the mineral springs seemed a perfect recipe for success. And for awhile it was. But in 1935, under somewhat mysterious circumstances, the hotel burned down and was not rebuilt.

Ownership of the land and the cabins along the creek reverted to the U.S. Forest Service. The Forest Service kept the property as it was, selling only the cabins and leasing, with a good number of restrictions, the land they sat on; land that abuts a 5,963 acre wilderness area. That a brewing company would build a hotel in the wilderness seems odd. That the government would enforce buffers that prevented the logging of valuable timber seems unusual. In fact, I find the whole thing magical.

And so, over the decades, for almost 100 years now, families have come and gone. A few of the cabins, destroyed by wind or fire or rot, have been rebuilt—but always within the original footprint. Most of the old cabins remain, however, carefully repaired and deeply loved.

The cabin in this story, the one just 10 feet or so from the burbling creek, has owners who visit often, driving in when the weather permits and skiing in in winter, carrying supplies in backpacks and sometimes pulling a sled. In spring and summer they hike and wade in the creek and pick huckleberries for pancakes. And on cool nights they build a fire in the outdoor fire pit and sit around it with a glass of wine, visiting. Sometimes they tell ghost stories or roast marshmallows or make smores. The smoke from the fire rises high and yet higher, till it reaches the height of the great trees whose tops disappear in the deepening night.

The forest floor is thick and dark, and the trees dwarf the cabin and the people around the campfire. The creek splashes and sings. An owl hoots; a distant dog barks once. The people are quiet, the night silent. But the silence is suffused with life, from tiny microbes to insects, to black bears, to the giant firs themselves, while the myriad plants of the understory hold hands beneath the surface of the forest floor, communicating that all is well. And this too is magic.

Washing rugs

Summer, 2014

If you've read our book, *Tea & Bee's Milk,* you know that we visited Turkey several times and lived there for a year. As a result we fell captive to the beauty of Turkish rugs and brought several home. Since we try to live simply it's rather embarrassing to admit we have five kilims (flat-weave rugs) and three knotted rugs. Since our house has no room for such bounty, two are loaned out. The others are on our floors or under our bed—and they were long overdue for a washing.

In Turkey such rugs are usually washed in a stream or lake and left to dry in the sun. I had no stream or lake but I did have an empty RV pad and a handy faucet. I also had lots of hot sun; perfect conditions in fact. I dragged the carpets outside, two at a time; filled a bucket with soapy water and a soft scrub brush and set to work. It was glorious.

I filled the brush and splashed it on the first kilim, moving slowly across the pattern and admiring again the handiwork of the woman, or possibly man, who had made it. If one is knowledgeable one can tell immediately where in Turkey a particular pattern was produced. I am not knowledgeable. But I loved the feeling of wet, hand-spun wool under my hands and knees, and I tried to imagine the weaver who had sat at her loom creating the geometric design that appeared, line by line before her.

This traditional art will someday pass, as technology takes over and weavers leave their villages to study and work and become "modern." In the meantime we are graced with lovely handmade rugs that warm my heart—still—each time I see them.

When I had finished scrubbing I turned on the hose. The water on my feet and legs was cooling in the 95 degree sun, and I probably rinsed longer than necessary. Then I called Ray to help me hang the rug on the fence to drip, and turned to the next one.

It took me two days to complete my task and when it was done I felt a great sense of accomplishment, along with a satisfying ache in my knees. Unease had fled.

As I write this, downtown Sisters is filled with hundreds of hanging quilts and many, many hundreds of people strolling the streets, taking pictures, taking notes, and appreciating the beauty of another kind of hand-made tapestry. This is the 40th anniversary of the Sisters Quilt Show and there's no lack of enthusiasm.

Art in any form is a human construct, made with eyes and hands. When the art those hands created connects with us—in the inexplicable way art does—it helps to keep us centered and content. Just as the simple housecleaning task of washing rugs relieved my stress and left me happy, so does a beautiful handmade object touch our hearts and make them sing. I love technology. But it will never make me as happy as an old Turkish kilim.

A cat in snow

November 2014

We have 15 inches of snow on the ground. It arrived three days ago and our view is essentially unchanged. Nothing is melting because it's 20 degrees outside. Despite the sunshine, which is abundant and beautiful, great clumps of snow still cling to the trees.

Yesterday we dug a trench to the street so we can walk to the market should the need arise. It hasn't, but it will before too much longer. This is more snow than Sisters usually gets at one time—at least that's what the natives say—but it's only half what we got last January. We hope we aren't seeing a pattern, because this much snow is hard on our backs.

Zoé, our cat, doesn't like it either. She ventured forth for the first time this afternoon and after she was gone two hours we began to wonder where she was. Of course calling a cat is useless unless they're already headed in your direction, so Ray (henceforth known as Pathfinder) put on his boots and set out to follow her trail. We both knew this was a waste of time, but it made us feel better.

Shortly after he went out the front door I spotted Zoé doing her balancing act along the back fence. Because the fence is narrow she can't walk atop it normally. Instead she uses her two left feet (or right, depending on direction) to walk along the fence top, while the other two travel along the horizontal brace that runs six inches lower. This bi-level locomotion is awkward even for a cat, but I have seen her run at a presentable speed when a squirrel was in view. Today, though, the fence was snowy and the going slow.

The trouble with getting yourself up on a fence is that no matter where you come down you're in 15 inches of snow. Clearly, this was not a welcome thought and Zoé meowed pitifully while navigating the fence's right turn toward the house. It seemed obvious that she would jump down when she got near the door but with typical cat logic she kept going. Ray eventually managed to catch up with her, and passed her through a nearby window to me. This move, which we considered a rescue, made her highly indignant. After complaining loudly and convincingly, she went off to wash herself. You can't win with a cat.

It's supposed to warm into the low 30s tomorrow and reach 40 by Tuesday. I expect this to improve Zoe's disposition. As for the humans in the family, I'm thinking a fire and a cognac might do it.

The balance of the day

December 2014

Today is my favorite day of the year. It's Winter Solstice, when the light returns and the days begin to lengthen. Earth itself appears to pause in its journey for about four days as it rests at aphelion— its farthest point from the sun. During these few days the earth is perfectly balanced between dark and light.

But here on the planet itself, with our feet on the ground and gravity to contend with, finding balance can be difficult. A child can learn to balance a bicycle, but living a balanced life is harder. We build mental constructs to justify or defend our actions to ourselves, to bolster our weak egos, or to conquer an old pain. These forms weigh heavily on one side or the other and cause us to slip, stumble, careen into places we don't want to be. In this rapidly changing world we are often mesmerized by events that throw us off balance, driving us to lean right or left, in defense or in fear.

The ponderosas here are typically tall, straight, and heavy, and they sit on a root structure that is shallow, except for the tap root. But some trees do lean. Today, on my morning walk, peering through rain-spotted glasses, I saw a tall pine, an old tree that had apparently been leaning since it was young. From my perspective on the path it tilted slightly to the right, and on that side I noticed that the branches were shorter than the ones on the left. The tree had grown more weight on its uphill side and thus achieved balance.

Nature is wise. She knows what needs to be done and she knows that all those random ideas and plans and worries that keep us tilting in one direction or another are nothing but chimeras. Unlike the ponderosas, who stand still on shallow roots, we can find balance simply by staying present and breathing. We are more complicated than trees but they are far more accepting—that is a lesson we can learn. Life is not a contest or challenge to be overcome. It's simply a chance to be here, on this Earth, circling the sun in a vast expanding universe. We can all pause and take a deep breath, and rest in the balance of this day.

So, how's your weather?

January 2015

When I opened my iPad and checked the weather app this morning I saw ten days of unusual warmth with no end in sight, coming after several weeks of temperatures mostly in the 40s. And this at 3,000 ft elevation, at the foot of 10,000+ ft mountains, in January. This is not a typical winter.

I was thinking about this when I took my walk this morning. I looked at the tall pines and wondered if they would still be here a 100 years hence, or dead from heat and disease. I thought about the great reservoirs of underground water that feed the lovely Metolius and McKenzie Rivers, and imagined fishermen dropping their lines into isolated pools of stagnant water surrounded by the rocky debris of once great streams. I passed a small herd of deer munching dead grass and thought about our little town without them.

We know that occasional weather events, like our unusual winter temperatures, are not evidence of global climate change. But if we're paying attention we also know that these changes have been increasing at an ever faster rate. The storms are bigger and more destructive, the temperatures more extreme. While the eastern half of the U.S. freezes, the southern hemisphere is suffering through an extended heat wave. In Australia, a hundred thousand bats dropped dead from heat up to 122 degrees Fahrenheit. Parrots, emus, and kangaroos are also dying from the heat. This is not a typical summer.

A recent report on Desmogblog.com, a popular site that tracks scientific climate research and related stories, indicates that out of 2,258 peer-reviewed climate articles by 9,136 authors, only one writer rejected man-made global warming. In a previous analysis the author, James Lawrence Powell, found that in 13,950 peer-reviewed articles between 1991 and 2012, just 24 scientists rejected global warming. He even offers his Excel spreadsheet of articles in case anyone wants to refute his analysis.

I don't want to refute it; I want to do something about it. But what? Wind and solar energy are helping (witness Germany's success with solar energy) and Americans are driving less. But that isn't going to change things quickly enough. We're still allowing and subsidizing companies who do fracking and oil drilling. Coal is still being mined and shipped and burned. We haven't raised taxes on gasoline, or invested in clean, efficient mass transit. There's no political will to take meaningful action on this or any other problem facing us. It's beyond frustrating.

I love our planet. I love being outdoors. I love walking through wildness, listening to the quiet, and surrendering my worries to the magic of a wild river, forest, desert or seashore. Nature is one of our greatest blessings. That we have apparently withdrawn our protection of this gift leaves me deeply saddened.

What are we to do?

As time goes by

Summer, 2015

I often feel I don't have enough time. But what does it really mean, to have time? In Einstein's world time is relative. It's the fourth dimension, intricately linked to space itself—spacetime. In the non-relativistic world, our world, time is treated as a constant, but it never feels constant to me. In my world the clock ticks ever so slowly or far too fast.

We learn early to succumb to the demands of the clock; we unquestioningly accept its rule. But our willingness to live by its precepts feels oddly mistaken. Have we trapped ourselves by our devotion to time and clocks and time clocks and efficiency and productivity?

Whenever I could I turned my back on those demands. I've loved many jobs while regretting the time I needed to give them. I never wanted my precious hours to go to a career, a company, or a boss. Which probably explains why my retirement is so meager! But it seemed to me—and still does—that this life, every life, deserves to be honored by filling its allotted days with what one values; not by exercising the skills that others value—even when well paid for them. Sometimes those values overlap, of course, but that is a rare and wonderful thing.

Henry David Thoreau said, "You must live in the present, launch yourself on every wave, find your eternity in each moment." I'm with Henry. We need and deserve time to sit, watch, listen, enjoy.

In America finding such time is difficult. Unlike most countries in the world the U.S. has zero national requirements for vacations or holidays. Most European countries designate 30 days of paid vacation, and employees are required to take it. With holidays, Austrians got 38 and Brazilians 41 paid days off in 2014. Yet many Americans work multiple jobs and get no days off, while being called lazy by vacation-loving politicians.

This is not a healthy way to live, and the discord, anger, and division we see around us are, I think, a direct consequence of valuing productivity—and capitalism—over life itself.

•

Whether we measure time in days, seasons, or decades, we are always paying homage to it. We do things from time to time, are present for the time being, will be there in no time, arrive in good time, and are frequently behind the times.

I expect we've all had the experience of time stretching as we travel. The strangeness of everything we see makes each moment unique, and the moment that follows behind it will contain some other uniqueness, some sight never seen, aroma never breathed, words never heard. Three weeks can feel like three months when everything is new. And then we return home to friends, excited about the stories we have to tell, and they say, "What, back already? Didn't you just leave?" Nothing deflates the eager story teller so quickly—which may be a good thing.

What contracts time, it seems to me, is habit, routine, and activities done mindlessly. Driving a well known route, you blink and realize you're at your destination and wonder how you got there. Your travel and time are lost in the fog of automaticity, the antithesis of mindfulness.

But no matter how we shape it or cut it or use it or ignore it, time will never retreat. It may stretch or bend itself beyond understanding, but as long as we're on earth, time will be with us. We are nothing without it. For what is life but time?

When in doubt, adapt

October 2015

Like many of you, my life has been a cascading series of events punctuated by change, indecision, surprise, misadventure, and downright craziness. Not to mention the primaries, which leave me wondering if America will survive the coming year.

When we came to Sisters we hoped it would be our last move. But we are now summoning the courage to put our house on the market once more and move back to the Portland area. Ray's illness is the primary reason; there are more care options there, and opportunities to participate in research. And of course our family and old friends will be much closer.

As I wrote the above paragraph I found myself wondering if this move is really what I want, and I have no answer. I will certainly hate leaving Sisters and the friends I've made here, but mostly I'll miss the nearby mountains and my walks through the pines, and the sunshine and dry weather—though it's snowing as I write this.

Through all our many moves (19 if you count France and Turkey) I have learned to be adaptable, finding something to love in each of our habitats, even when the surroundings were less than lovely. I am not alone in this of course. The world is a shifting mass of humanity, most fleeing war, terror, economic collapse, or other misfortunes. With no other choice they are forced to adapt to new surroundings, a new culture, a new language. In contrast, our moves have generally been our decision, our choice.

Adaptation is a key survival mechanism and the millions of refugees adapting to new surroundings offer proof of that. As we adapt we adopt new ideas, new societal norms; and we share old traditions with our new neighbors. All this is good in the long run, but it isn't easy. Personally, I'm growing tired of the turmoil. I would like the world to rest awhile, to reach a kind of stasis, so we can all plant deep roots; roots that will hold us and our surroundings in place for a time, providing continuity, solace, permanence, and hope.

But I could be wrong. Maybe upset and constant churning are good for us. Maybe adapt is just another way of saying evolve. And maybe our politics will return to normal and our endless wars will cease. One can always hope. And if that fails, adapt.

Autumn Redux

October 2015

The flowers in my garden are fading, but the trees are gold and red and brighten the view from inside the house. The sun still shines daily, but mornings are cold and walks are postponed until temperatures rise. I want to spend every waking moment out in the weakening sunshine. To hell with housework, to hell with musts and shoulds. I will take a good book into the yard and the sun, and read until sunset.

But of course I don't. Like most people I stick to routine—though mine I confess is loose. Still, I do what's expected of me, what needs to be done, and if there's any time left in the day I sit down at the computer and read email and the news, while the good book lies unopened on the table. Am I the only one who short-circuits my own best interests? I think not.

This sunshine, this paler, less intense sister to summer sun, is a joyful blessing, holding off with outstretched hands the cold winter days it presages. I stare out the window at the fading blossoms and wonder why autumn, this season of slow decay, brings with it so much color and beauty, as though celebrating the coming sleep. What is the scientific rationale for all this color? Why this glorious curtain call? What was the creator thinking?

Fall is also, of course, the season of beginnings. For no matter how long we have been away from school, that annual urge to begin the year anew tugs at us from somewhere deep in our consciousness, and if I was smart I'd use that urge to delve deeper, to try new ideas, to start new projects—or even finish old ones. The leaves outside may be dying but inside I can metaphorically turn over a new one and try again to do better.

But not yet. Not quite yet. Now, at this moment, I will take up that unread book and move into that paler sun. It won't last much longer and when it fades into rainclouds and winter, then I'll explore those new ideas. I will! I promise.

This interesting world

November 2015

"May you live in interesting times," states the mythical Chinese curse, and without doubt we do. Until the last decade I thought living in interesting times would be fun and exciting. Now I'm not so sure. The world is changing so quickly that even the calmest among us feels agitated and anxious. Before we can catch up with the events of last week, they have spun into newer more complex versions of themselves. We are lost in a sea of uncertainty while the worries of tomorrow lay in wait.

This interesting world is one we created and must now take responsibility for. We must conquer frustration and impatience and our own ignorance and solve our problems, including the most pressing, climate change—before which all other problems fade to oblivion. What good are your devices if no network exists, if there is no food or fresh water, if your home is under water, if the Gulf Stream has quit streaming?

Naomi Klein is a Canadian writer who gave six years and a great deal of thought to the problem of global climate change, and I recommend her book, *This Changes Everything*. It's not an easy book, but you will be glad you read it. There is also a documentary film by the same name.

Klein's book reminds us in heart-wrenching ways that this interesting world, this beautiful, endlessly fascinating globe spinning through space, is our only home, and we must protect it with the same strength and energy we protect our children or ourselves. There are ways to do this if we act quickly and with collective strength, and her well-documented book is an excellent resource, a good place to start.

But what we also need to do, I think, in addition to marching and writing letters and donating money, and paddling kayaks in opposition to Shell, is to remind ourselves of our selves—or our souls if you prefer. Our disconnect from Earth has grown slowly over time. Conveniences like electric light and steam generation; and coal, oil and gas, and now the digital revolution, enticed us away from Earth's natural pace and rhythm. But ever so gently, so that now we hardly notice how alienated—and destructive—we have become.

I am lucky to have easy access to the natural world and I have learned that if I pay attention it will speak to me. The caw of a raven, the sound of wind through the firs, the sudden bolt of a young deer, all work to bring me back to the present. Suddenly I am out of my head and back on the path, aware of the now. Nature is willing to help us if we only pay attention.

And while a charming landscape is helpful, it's not required. We can attend while sitting in front of our always captivating screens by simply remembering that we are alive; that we are in the world Now. We may not like where we are but what matters is that we acknowledge the moment, that fleeting moment that is gone before you can name it. Life and Earth are gifts, and acknowledging that, however briefly, serves us all.

Portland, Again

In late February, 2016 we called a real estate agent and put our Sisters home on the market. It was, I think, the toughest decision we ever made. Ray was still able to contribute his ideas and opinions but he was fading quickly and I felt the need to be settled while he was still aware of his surroundings. The house sold immediately.

We moved to Portland in late April, but it was the end of June before we settled into our condominium, and our new life. Ray was taking part in a drug study at Oregon Health Science University and it was then we learned that he had Lewy body/Parkinson's, a combination predicting a much faster progression. I soon became a full time caregiver.

It's inevitable

I've been doing a lot of painting since we moved into our little condo. I like painting but it's harder than it used to be. Squatting and reaching and bending for hours is hard on my aging body. But I take another ibuprofen and keep painting, because I am driven to make this space ours as quickly as I can. The paint roller moves and the old, washed-out colors—the betraying evidence of another's life—disappear. Instant affirmation; I am here.

Our condo was built in the early 90s and has no doubt had many owners. The most recent before ourselves did some upgrading: new appliances, new sinks, new cabinets in kitchen and baths. For the most part I like what they did, but the need to make it mine is strong. Hence the painting, new lights, and new gas fireplace.

This need to paper over other's choices can sometimes cause problems. I vividly remember the day the former owner of our very first house decided to drop in unexpectedly. He seemed very ancient to my late 20s eyes. I think now he was probably about 80. He and his wife had lived in the house for many years and he was homesick. So he came home again, to the place that held his happiness.

But that place no longer existed. Appalled by a dining-room wall papered with ducks that flew straight at you, we had torn them off, just as we had the floral paper in the living room. The interior was freshly painted and the kitchen wore new linoleum. The poor man was as appalled as we had been by the duck wallpaper. I tried to talk to him, to explain that it was our first house, that we wanted it to feel like ours, that we loved the house—and all the other things one might say to a distraught, elderly gentleman. It was no use. He left in tears, grateful that his wife had not come along. I felt like crying with him.

It was a good lesson though.

Dwellings are highly personal and unique to their owners in ways that even frequent visitors can't recognize. This is as it should be. But leaving such a home is a wrench. It takes time for an unfamiliar empty shell to capture and absorb one's personal uniqueness, to be a stage for one's personal narrative. Belonging arrives slowly, in fits and starts, but with effort it does arrive.

And so I'll keep painting until I've covered every wall, every corner, every baseboard, determinedly putting our stamp on this unfamiliar shell where we reside. And the day will come when I look around and suddenly feel that we are truly home again. It may take awhile, but it's inevitable.

Transitions

September 2016

It rained all day yesterday and some of the leaves just off our balcony turned from pale pink to dark red. I guess fall is here. It will be interesting to see what happens to our view as the weeks roll by. At the moment we see the variegated greens of many deciduous trees—almost touchable from the balcony wall—and here and there in the background, an evergreen. I imagine we'll feel quite exposed when all these leaves depart, but maybe not. There are so many trees it's almost like a forest.

There's a real forest just a hop away. It's Portland's Forest Park, at 5,157 acres the largest urban forest park in the U.S. Our condo complex sits near the edge of Forest Park and sometimes it's hard to remember that we live just three miles from downtown, with all its busyness and bustle. There are 80 miles of trails in the park so when the pain in my Achilles tendon lets up there are plenty of opportunities for good walks.

It's lovely having nature near at hand and it helps make the transition from small town to city a bit easier. But it's still a transition. I still miss the ponderosas. And from experience I know it takes a least a year to feel like you belong in a new place. And this move has actually brought us to two places, one that can be found on a map and one that can't. Ray's illness has brought us both to a whole new country.

I don't want to write about his disease. There are plenty of books and articles, and blogs no doubt, about it. I don't intend to contribute to that. But it's important to acknowledge, and to accept that it has changed our lives. Ray is still in the early stages but it has affected his mobility and his attitude. He's no longer the curious, outgoing, eager-for-life guy I've known so many years. He's quieter and less interested in the world. But he still has his quirky sense of humor. And we still laugh a lot.

This transition is going to be slower and harder, but it will come. Life is truly a gift, and the lessons the universe keeps thrusting on me are unchanging and wise: Be treelike. Accept and do your best. Open your heart. Forgive others and yourself. And love, love, love.

I'm not angry am I?

February, 2017

I've been having jaw trouble, or TMJ, for those who prefer exactness. This is not new, it's been recurring since I was a teenager and is often caused by stress. Most of the time it repairs itself quickly, but it's been hanging around too long, and is annoying and sometimes painful.

Searching for answers to "why is this happening?" I picked up an old book by Louise Haye that a friend gave me years ago. It contains an alphabetical list of body parts and their common ailments, with what Hayes believes are the root causes of such ailments—usually spiritual or stress-related. I've found this list to be both accurate and dead wrong so I keep it for entertainment, and also because in a few instances the insight provided relief.

I flipped through the pages and found "jaw problems" followed by "anger and resentment." Hmmm, I thought, I don't think so. I don't feel angry, and certainly not resentful.

"You missed this one," I told Louise as I replaced the book and went back to my work. It was somewhat mindless work and inevitably I thought again about her diagnosis. Do I feel angry? I began to think that maybe I did. Maybe soon evolved to yes, and once I acknowledged that, the anger came roaring forth, surprising me with its strength. Indeed, I was shocked by my lack of self-knowledge, for as soon as I conceded the emotion I found I was angry at everything.

I was angry with Ray for being ill. I was angry at doctors and scientists who denied him a cure. I was angry at the cat for scratching the furniture. I was angry with myself for my incompetence as a caregiver. I was angry that I had a new car but only seemed to drive to doctor's offices. The anger began with me and extended to family members, friends, and the wide world of politics. Not surprisingly, much of it bore the presidential seal.

The force of this suppressed rage shocked me, and as new recognitions surfaced I wept cathartic tears. By day's end I felt better; even lighter. I sat down and wrote a list beginning "I am angry that..." It covered three pages in a small notebook. Then I ripped them out and burned them in the kitchen sink. And then I wrote a list of all the things that make me happy, grateful, and loved. That one I'm keeping.

Anger is not always a bad thing. It is often required—think of righteous anger—and it can move us to action. But action driven by anger needs careful monitoring, and seething anger can kill us and others. To give it credit, however, anger is a legitimate emotion, unlike guilt and jealousy which serve no purpose except to make us miserable.

No matter how cathartic my experience, how extensive the anger expelled, this was only a partial purge. With the world in such a state how could it not be? Anger is justified. But I have learned a lesson. Now I will seek to recognize, manage, and release—not suppress it. Because with anger gone there's a lot more room for love.

Memorial Day

May 2017

A gray morning. I open the *New York Times* site and see a photo of endless white crosses on a grassy slope. It makes me wonder; if we could add up every life lost in every U.S. war and action and evacuation and operation, how many would there be? Thousands? Hundreds of thousands? Millions?

Curious, I turn to Google, which shows me copies of every document officially declaring war. There are eleven. Great Britain in 1812, Spain and Mexico in 1846, Austria-Hungary and Germany in 1917 (WWI), and of course WWII, when we declared war on Japan, Germany, and Italy in December 1941 and Bulgaria, Romania, Hungary in June 1942.

But then something happened. Declared war became a thing of the past—a strange deviation for a country so in love with its military. Now we just have actions, or operations, or incursions, or sometimes evacuations.

I turned to Wikipedia and found a list of every action in which the U.S. participated (including a few for humanitarian purposes). Of course anyone of my generation immediately thinks of Vietnam, nine years of misery and a sundering of our unity. In reality it was longer than that, there were military advisers in South Vietnam as early as 1959. But before Vietnam there was Korea 1950–1953, and through the 50s the U.S. involved its military eight times in sites around the world.

In the 1960s the count rises to ten: two Cuban actions, an expeditionary force landing in Thailand, planes to Congo, advisers to Laos; Dominican Republic, Laos again, Cambodia, a few more.

The slow rise continues into the 1970s, when there are 11; mostly endlessly continuing actions in Vietnam, Cambodia, Korea. But in the 1980s the number explodes to 29 and includes such names as "operation Earnest Will, operation Praying Mantis, and operation Prime Chance. A few of these last more than a year. These names make me think the military is having too much fun.

In the 1990s the list expands again to 32, again with several multi-year actions. From 2000 to 2009 it drops to 20, including the war in Afghanistan, the war in Iraq, and the war on terror—all of which continue to this day. (Note that though we call them wars, Congress, the only body with responsibility for declaring war, didn't.)

The list from 2010 to 2017 shows 22 actions, but by now I am too depressed to go on. And I've not touched the Civil War, the slave rebellions, the battles against Native Americans.

So the answer to my question, "how many" is an obvious "far, far too many." And looking at this long list one has to ask, how many died for a useless cause, a mistake, a regretted decision? And how many of these events could have been avoided with a little less testosterone and a lot more talk?

There will always be reasons to fight. But I hope that in the not too distant future we'll avoid unnecessary deaths, and instead assume humanity's capacity to solve problems without resorting to weapons. We will have to exchange our love of guns and glory for devotion to common sense and creative thinking. We can do that. And to honor all those millions who have died for us, we must.

The complexity of loss

May, 2017

A few weeks ago blue jays started building a nest in a tree outside our window and I looked forward to seeing tiny birds take their first flying lessons. But the blue jays have deserted us. Maybe they decided having a nest so near a cat wasn't wise (it's just five or six feet from the balcony perch the cat prefers), but Zoé would run in fear at two jays squawking and flapping their wings in her direction. Surely they knew this.

I took the binoculars out yesterday and looked closely at the nest. No sign of life at all. The piled sticks and leaves hugged the tree's trunk—a habit of jays—and the nest, like a sloppily-made basket, was the perfect size for a large bird and a couple of chicks. The loss made me feel lonely, which is ridiculous since I'd had no chance to make their acquaintance; let alone know their names. But still, it was a loss.

The casual complexity of the nest reminded me of other complexities, the life cycle of the frogs I hear chirping in the undergrowth, and the fractal geometry contained within the tree leaves that I can almost touch if I lean over the balcony rail. These are hints of the deep complexities that form our world and I am in awe when I spend time looking and listening.

It is these complexities that worry me when I think of climate change. It's impossible for us to know—let alone understand—the interrelationships between ourselves and the millions of species that share our planet. It's easy to be distraught over the loss of polar bears, but what about the 300,000 species of beetles? Don't they deserve a little sympathy?

We all know the doleful litany—denuded forestlands, acidic oceans, loss of cultivable land, poisoned air—all interlocking complexities, all produced by humans. No bee, beetle, bear, or bird created this catastrophe but they suffer it regardless. If we cannot stop the warming we leave these creatures confronting mass extinction. And all the vital complexities contained within them, all the still unknown interlocking pieces of our world, pieces that might solve problems we don't even have yet, will die with them.

I don't want to wake up one morning to find no birds in my trees, no bees buzzing around the lavender, no butterflies flitting across the landscape. I hope the jays will come back next spring and try again. I hope there will always be jays and that spring will always come round to warm and delight us with the colors and sounds and complexities of nature. I doubt humans can live without that, and I don't think I want to.

In wildness I trust

July, 2017

We spent Saturday in the woods at a little cabin beside a creek. It's an easy drive from Portland but the highway carries you into another realm. Tall, old-growth Douglas firs surround the cabin, and a wilderness area is within easy reach. No internet signal intrudes. There is water, but no electricity.

Ray sat on the porch and watched his granddaughter practice her carving skills while the creek burbled through low rapids a few feet away. I went for a walk. It felt good to be back among the trees and I walked slowly, enjoying the feeling that wooded areas always inspire in me, that of being among friends. I stopped often to look up, sometimes resting my hand on a tree so I wouldn't fall over as I leaned back to see the tops of the firs so far above me, their branches swaying in the breeze against a pale blue sky.

The dirt track I followed was more like a trail than a road, quite narrow in places, and strewn with pine needles and crushed cones. The understory was thick with ferns, a few white daisies and tiny pink flowers that I couldn't identify; some Oregon grape, a blackberry bush. But the ferns ruled.

About thirty minutes in I crossed a barrier into the wilderness area and stopped at the sign-in box that marks all such boundaries. Parties of up to 12 are permitted, I read, but those 12 include livestock—horses presumably, or maybe llamas—and it made me smile to see this conflating of humans and livestock—a rare thing in our human-centric world.

I didn't sign in; I was only going a short distance, to the creek that I could easily hear and was tempted to cross. But jumping from wet rock to wet rock didn't seem prudent out here in the lonesome so I took a longing look at the narrow path through the trees beyond and turned back.

At the cabin our hosts were headed to the swimming hole to see who could stay in the icy water the longest. I eased myself into a hammock strung between two trees at the edge of the creek. Gazing upward I saw nothing but pale green leaves lit by sunlight, of vine maple and alder, and higher, another kind of maple. Beyond that were glimpses of blue and the tip of a fir tree.

As I lay there I thought about all those—especially children—who live without ever experiencing a day in the woods, a dip in a cold creek, or even a walk along a pine-cone strewn road. This saddened me, because such moments are magical and touched with spirit, intangible but crucial. Without spirit we are simply egocentric beings marching to the drumbeat of culture and society. With it, we are the world and everything in it, even the universe itself.

There are those who would steal nature from us, to kill and drill and log and mine for money. They cannot take all of it, but they may try, and we must resist. Our day on the creek was a welcome break from city life. But the best part was knowing there are more forests and lakes and rivers and oceans—and all the life contained within them—just over the horizon. And all are waiting for us until needed again. May it always be so.

A dose of physics

July 2017

There's nothing better to heal the stress of current societal turmoil than a dose of physics. To spend an hour in the submicroscopic realm of quarks and photons, of spin clouds and quanta, is to leave the irksome deeds of the macroscopic world far behind.

I've been enjoying just that while reading *Reality is Not What it Seems: The Journey to Quantum Gravity*, by Italian physicist Carlo Rovelli. The author's first sentence pulled me in, for he describes a journey from Miletus to Abdera in the year 450 BCE. I have stood among the ruins of Miletus, in Turkey, and tried to imagine the great city as it once was. Rovelli's purpose, however, was to introduce us to Democritus of Abdera, the first atomist. Everything, he believed, was made of atoms, indivisible, freely moving in space.

From there the author introduces, in succession, the great physicists and their ideas, from Isaac Newton, to Einstein, Neils, Werner, and more. It's a very readable book, and I recommend it. You don't need to understand loop quantum gravity or quantum mechanics (no one does) to appreciate that the world is both more complex, and simpler, than what we imagine. In fact quantum gravity predicts that the world is made of only one thing: covariant quantum fields. Try that on for size.

The search for quantum gravity is really the search for a unified theory, a way of understanding how both Einstein's general relativity and quantum mechanics—very different concepts—explain the same universe. Rovelli believes they are close to proving such a theory, while also admitting it may never be found. But science progresses, and if you can believe that space is granular, that entangled particles communicate instantaneously across vast distances, and that time exists only when heat is present, you are half way there.

I willingly accept all this, but I'm puzzled most about consciousness. Quantum physics says that quanta exist as both particles and waves in a field of potentiality. That is, it is nowhere until observed, at which time it becomes a particle in a place—an electron in a light bulb for instance. This strange fact has been proven over and over again.

In laboratory experiments it is presumably a human who does the observing. But can the observer also be a machine? An animal? An insect? And how does the wave/particle know that it is or has been observed? Is it conscious? Does it recognize other consciousness? Is consciousness required in order for the world to exist? Is our collective consciousness creating reality around us? And what the heck is consciousness?

No one knows that either, apparently. I once read a book titled *The Physics of Consciousness,* hoping to learn the secret. Alas, it turns out the author didn't know, though he had a lot of interesting ideas.

I love physics. It's incredibly challenging and I admit I don't comprehend all that I read, but it opens my mind in ways that nothing else does. Rovelli says that physics is like fresh air through an open window. I like that. If you're depressed about the state of the country or the world I can't think of a better antidote. Reach for a physics book and take a deep dive. You may find the world is a place of endless potentiality. What could be better?

A perfect life

September, 2017

There is smoke in the air again today, so instead of the patio I am comfortably settled on the living room couch. Since we've hardly used this room all summer it feels odd and is a distinct reminder that winter, and use of the fireplace, aren't far off. The week ahead promises to be rainy, which adds to the sense of summer's end.

While I write Ray is in the spare room watching a rerun of a bike race in Spain. Both of us are enjoying this day without plans because the week has been unusually busy. Tuesday it was the bath aide and a sitter, so I could run errands for three hours. Wednesday it was two women to talk about the caregiver study I agreed to participate in (my contribution to science). Thursday brought a speech therapist to check on Ray's swallowing (one of the symptoms of Lewy body). Among other things she suggested thickened water. Ick. Friday was the bath aide again, plus a PT to help with transfers. She watched as I helped Ray move from wheelchair to couch, and said my technique was excellent. I felt like a kid getting an unexpected A.

All this attention to illness is not unexpected but it lays bare how much our life is consumed by it. As Ray grows less able to care for himself I take up the slack, but while I grow more intimately aware of his most basic needs, I understand less and less of his thinking. The two issues are on divergent paths and the distances between them grow daily. Communication suffers, of course, but I have learned to shorten my sentences, to cease sharing complicated topics, to hear silence in answer to questions. Instead of talking to Ray I talk out loud to myself, and sometimes wonder if I too am not losing all sense.

Next week the every-other-week nurse will return, as will the bath aide and the PT—this time to work on car transfers. All bring a whiff of the outside world with them along with their help and conversation. I will be here, chopping wood and carrying water, and living in the now with Ray and the cat. It is not an exciting life, but it is not to be disparaged. It is the perfect life for me, at this moment, now.

Changes

November 2017

I once admired a pin that a friend was wearing, and when I retired she gave it to me. It's an artistic little thing made of copper and brass; a bar with three metal hearts and a single word suspended by loops below: *Change.* Shannon died a few months ago, but the pin is on my jacket and I think of her every time I see it.

Change is something we all live with. Some welcome it and others dread it, but no matter how we feel about it, it's a powerful motivator. I've always tried to welcome change even when negative, because it carries with it such valuable lessons. For me the word has usually meant new vistas, new friends, new beginnings. *Change.*

There are other kinds of change of course. There's entropy (brought to us by the second law of thermodynamics) which tells us all things decline, disintegrate, fall apart. Organization decays into chaos, plates break, walls crumble, and where concrete erodes, weeds sprout and flowers bloom. Entropy is everywhere and humans are prime examples. No matter how we fight it, we age, decline, and die. Since I'm writing this on my birthday that idea has a special poignancy. *Change.*

I have witnessed a great deal of change in the last eight weeks, which is one reason I haven't been here writing. My husband is now on hospice. This alone feels shocking, and the change has brought a bevy of new people into our lives, caregivers of every kind and miscellaneous others. The phone rings far more than it ever has, and my alone time has shrunk markedly. *Change.*

I try not to think ahead to the great change that is coming, but at times I find myself slipping into daydreams, mostly about how nice it will be when the hospital bed, lift, table, and two wheel-chairs are removed from our small premises. I regret these thoughts but humans are essentially selfish; I refuse to feel guilty.

In the broader world we are faced with as-tonishing, even shocking changes that were un-imaginable until they weren't. I can do little about that either, except heap praise on those fighting to uphold the norms and laws that we all took for granted before 2016. The pace of change is no longer a stately and steady altering, but a clock warping slide toward dystopia. We can only hang on and try to remember that change is good. It is opportunity, it is possibility, it is life and it is death. We might as well welcome it. *Change.*

Mourning Ray

11:29 February 9, 2018

It is exactly a week since Ray died. I have been crying off and on all morning while going about my chores; breakfast, shower, picking up, doing dishes, feeding the cat. It has been much the same all week. But what do I feel? I can't decipher it. Sadness, yes; loss, certainly; longing of course; wondering. Where is he? What is he doing now? Does he know I'm still here? Has he lost all interest in Earth and its drama?

And what am I to do now? That's the real question, and the only one I can answer, though not now; not yet. Now I can only keep going, keep putting one foot in front of the other, though moving that foot has little meaning.

In an effort to return to normal I went to Costco yesterday, my regular monthly trip, and half way down the first aisle I realized I was buying for one. It was like being hit on the head with a pillow; a numbing reminder. What was I doing there? Can one shop for one at Costco? Yes, one can, but not often.

Ray's death was long in coming. I saw hints of approaching dementia as early as 2012, though I blew them off as simply aging, or anxiety, or lack of sleep. I had many excuses, and in fact such hints were far apart and not terribly obvious. It was on a trip in 2014, after a series of mini disasters that Ray couldn't seem to handle, that I was sure. Later that year he was diagnosed with Alzheimer's. Unfortunately that diagnosis was later changed to Lewy bodies, a combination of dementia and Parkinson's—a double hit on the brain, as a nurse would tell me, and therefore a faster progression.

So I sit here at the computer, writing because it's the only thing I can think to do. Writing words that mean nothing without the context of the man himself, a kind, compassionate, smart, witty man with whom I was privileged to share a life of laughter and curiosity and adventure. He wasn't perfect and I didn't expect him to be, but he loved life and hated injustice, and he wasn't afraid to speak his truth whenever he saw the need. I learned a great deal from him, but I will never be as good, as kind, or as funny.

And now one week without Ray is behind me, and the next one looms as empty and sterile as a waiting petrie dish. I will put one foot in front of the other because I must.

Here's to the caregivers

March 2018

March is Women's History Month and today is International Women's Day. I've spent the morning vacuuming, dusting, and cleaning the kitchen because Laura is coming for tea.

I had thought of honoring women in my family this month, for women's history is essentially the history of our families. There are many I could draw on, from those who supported the underground railroad, to the sisters who fought for women's rights alongside Cady Stanton and Susan B. Anthony.

Closer to home I could write about my paternal grandmother, who raised eight children on an Oklahoma homestead and wrote poetry, and kept a pet pig that she washed every laundry day in the big cast-iron cauldron that now sits in my daughter's living room, full of throws.

I met Alice Hedglin Coffin only a few times and most of my memories are of tales others told. Like the time she found a large rattlesnake asleep on the floor of the parlor. Alice grabbed the shotgun that was always nearby and threw it over the snake. Then she planted a foot on each end of the gun and called for help. A son soon appeared and cut off the snake's head. Then he asked, "Why didn't you just shoot it?" for Alice was as good as any man with a gun.

"Because I didn't want holes in the floor!" she replied. Which always made sense to me.

In the end though, I decided not to write about family; that can wait. Today I want to honor the women who too often go unsung and under-paid. I had the good fortune to know several over the last months of Ray's life. Sometimes they came when called, like Syri, who lived down the hill and filled in when others couldn't make it. Sometimes they came for an hour or two a week, like the nurses; or twice weekly, like the bath aides. And sometimes they were there every day. One of these, Laura, was with me the longest, eight hours a day toward the end.

Laura had worked with dementia patients for nine years, and with those in hospice for the last six. She was knowledgeable, competent, kind, and loving. She cooked scrambled eggs for Ray, with the hot peppers he loved. When he could no lon-ger hold a spoon she fed him, and when he could no longer eat she gave him hourly doses of mor-phine to ease the pain of inevitable bed sores. We bonded over dirty diapers and strong cups of green tea. I heard about her extended family and the tra-ditions of her Mexican roots, and she heard stories of our travels and my highly opinionated views on politics. I could not have gotten through the last months without her.

Most women become caregivers at some time in their life, but few make careers of it and those few—there may be millions in the US alone—deserve our respect, decent pay, and even honor. So today, on International Women's Day, I'm happy to honor and thank them. And I'm also happy because Laura is coming for tea.

So many lessons

April, 2018

Writing here a year ago I cited T.S. Eliot's famous line, "April is the cruelest month" while complaining about the constant rain. This year is no different. Each morning I check my weather app hoping to see sunny skies in the future, and each morning I see rain predicted ten days hence. I think I should stop doing this.

My new life continues to evolve and the days have taken on a kind of habitualness that has the benefit of filling the hours, if nothing else. My concentration has improved enough that I can now sit for a half hour with a book without reading the same sentence endlessly, or battling the omni-present urge to do something else. Even the news doesn't hold much interest, and for a news junky that is weird. But the president and I have this in common; we are both living through a depressing year. The difference is, he doesn't know it.

So what have I learned so far from this year of bereavement? I have learned that by flitting from one task to another a lot can be accomplished. The satisfaction of actually finishing something, how-ever, is missing. I have learned that yogurt can be eaten for breakfast, lunch, and dinner; that errands can be put off indefinitely; and that the body can produce an endless amount of tears. Thanks to my grief counselor I have learned that talking to yourself out loud is neither unusual nor a sign of imminent dementia. This was a relief.

I have learned that I can still laugh out loud, still enjoy friends and outings, still look forward to events, while holding a sadness in my heart. I am impressed with the flexibility of my heart, how it makes room for boundless love and seemingly endless grief. If the rest of our bodies were as flexible as our hearts we would all be made of rubber.

Despite the evil and suffering that fills the world, I still believe we have within us the power to change. In ways big and small that is happening every day. And maybe my grief is its own wake up call. Today, life without Ray feels empty and meaningless. But I know in my flexible heart that more awaits, and that the years ahead will confirm what I've always known, that all life is a gift.

One year later

April, 2019

How to describe a year when nothing changes, but nothing is the same? Some days were quietly impossible, other days were filled with energy and hope. Some days I cried a lot, other days I laughed with friends. There is no pattern to grief, and that lack of pattern makes it confusing and difficult. Just when you think things are looking up, down you go.

A friend whose husband had died a year earlier told me the second six months were harder for her than the first, and I found that true as well. At first you're so busy with the details dying demands that you have little time to grieve. It was months before the agencies of the world stopped peppering me with questions and demanding attention. But they did keep me busy.

And then I was alone, without Ray's conversation and companionship. Alone was new. I had moved from my parent's home to roommates to marriage. Now I had to learn to be without Ray and with myself. And since I'm the cranky one it's been a bit of a challenge.

When I met with my grief counselor in January—yes, I'm still doing that—I complained that I had expected to be "well" by now and I wasn't.

And she laughed and said "You're never going to be *well*; you're going to be different." Changed. Which put an entirely new spin on the way I thought about my life.

Her remark was a small shove from the universe. A few days later I got a bigger one. It came via email. "Mom, here's a fare to Hong Kong for only $525 RT!"

In 1995 the fax from our friends in Turkey arrived at two in the morning. I stumbled into my office and carried it back to bed, where I read it aloud to Ray: the description of the available apartment, the timeframe, the cost. By the time we dropped off to sleep again we had said yes.

A famous Zen aphorism declares, "Leap and the net will appear." And for us it always did. We decided yes even when our goal seemed impossible, when the money wasn't there, or the time, or whatever. We held hands and leapt and the net appeared. But it was never an empty net. It was filled with tasks, like planning, organizing, saving, and often sacrificing. The door will open, the net will catch you, but you have to do the work.

After Ray died I thought I was finished with travel. I had no interest, made no plans, and if it came up in conversation I always said no. It wasn't that I was afraid of traveling alone; the familiar urge just wasn't there. At the suggestion of a friend I considered a writing/meditation workshop in Spain. The idea floated in my head for months, but when a decision was needed I could only say no.

And then that email arrived, and later this year I'm off to Hong Kong with a friend. It's a destination I had never considered, but the universe sent me that bargain fare, and the message was clear. It almost felt like an order. What could I do? I leapt. Now I'm excited and slightly terrified, but I'm back in planning mode, doing the work, checking off tasks. But still, I miss Ray's comforting presence.

I also miss his hugs, his conversation, and his cooking, and I will never stop loving him. But I've been given this gift of on-my-own time and it would be foolish to waste it. I'm not sure yet how or whether I've changed or who I'll ultimately turn out to be. But I will continue putting one foot in front of the other because I can. And because there's still so much to see.

Acknowledgements

Many people contributed to this book's final form and their help has been invaluable. Thank you to Joanne McClennan, an old friend and a willing critic—a valuable asset. Thanks to Nadine Fiedler, Sally Petersen, and Martha Ragland, who all contributed suggestions that greatly improved the final work. And thanks to my daughter Jennifer for her support and willingness to reread and reread. The ideas and opinions, as well as any errors, are my own.

Karen Gilden is a writer, editor, traveler, and tree lover whose articles have appeared in local and national publications. She is the author of four books, and has been blogging since 2006. She lives in Portland, Oregon.

Learn more, and subscribe to her blog at

karengilden.com

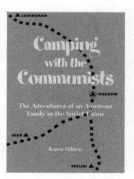
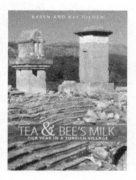

CPSIA information can be obtained
at www.ICGtesting.com
Printed in the USA
FSHW022003271019
63467FS